THE DON'T SWEAT GUIDE
FOR TEACHERS

Other books by the editors of Don't Sweat Press

The Don't Sweat Affirmations

The Don't Sweat Guide for Couples

The Don't Sweat Guide for Graduates

The Don't Sweat Guide for Grandparents

The Don't Sweat Guide for Parents

The Don't Sweat Guide for Moms

The Don't Sweat Guide for Weddings

The Don't Sweat Guide to Golf

The Don't Sweat Stories

The Don't Sweat Guide to Travel

The Don't Sweat Guide to Weight Loss

The Don't Sweat Guide to Taxes

The Don't Sweat Guide for Dads

The Don't Sweat Guide to Retirement

The Don't Sweat Guide for Newlyweds

THE DON'T SWEAT GUIDE
FOR TEACHERS

Cutting Through the Clutter
So That Every Day Counts

By the Editors of Don't Sweat Press
Foreword by Richard Carlson, Ph.D.

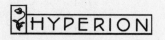

New York

Hyperion books are available for special promotions, premiums, or corporate training. For details contact Michael Rentas, Proprietary Markets, Hyperion, 77 West 66th Street, 12th floor, New York, New York 10023, or call 212-456-0133

ISBN-10: 0-7868-9053-3
ISBN-13: 978-0-7868-9053-8

FIRST EDITION

10 9 8 7 6 5

Contents

Foreword

Anyone who knows me, knows that I love and respect teachers as much as any other group of people. Without certain teachers in my life, my road would have been traveled in a very different way. I suspect this is true for anyone reading this book. I also acknowledge the important role many teachers have played in each of my two girls' educations, thus far. I'm not talking simply about their ability to teach the subjects, but the way they share their wisdom, compassion, time, energy, and love.

In my opinion, teachers have one of the most difficult and critical careers in the world. They should, by any standards, be revered and treasured. Unfortunately, that's not always the case. The simple truth is, many people don't know how difficult a job a teacher has.

So one of the obstacles a teacher must overcome is a feeling of being taken for granted. The good news is, although this is a real problem, it's also the case that we can train ourselves to take things less personally, and in doing so, stay true to our mission. As we mature, we discover that our own thinking and attitude play an enormous role in determining our fate in life—how we will react and how we will feel. It's our thinking that determines our level of wisdom; how we bounce back from adversity or criticism. To me, this is one of the key underlying lessons of this book.

I've spoken to hundreds of teachers during the course of my career. Many have shared with me that if they were somehow able to get over some of the "political" stuff and/or the parts where they were clearly being taken for granted, they would absolutely love the most important part—the teaching and the kids!

I think the editors of Don't Sweat Press have done an extraordinary job in this *Don't Sweat Guide for Teachers*. They have identified many of the issues that can create internal stress for teachers—yet they have also provided you with many excellent solutions. I encourage you to take a close look at those solutions and to take to heart those that apply to your life.

I'm very fond of this book and the way it has been presented. I admire the fact that you have chosen teaching as a career and as a way to give back to our world. Without you, we would be in deep trouble. You can feel secure that you have one very devoted fan— me. I hope this guide helps you create even more joy in what I believe is one of the most important jobs ever created.

Thanks again for your commitment to our young people. I send you my love and best wishes.

Richard Carlson
Benicia, California, 2003

THE DON'T SWEAT GUIDE
FOR TEACHERS

1.

Be Who You Are

What do you say when someone asks, "What do you do?" Strictly speaking, the accurate answer to what you do is, "I teach." But more often, you probably respond with, "I am a teacher." You identify your being with your professional activity. This is understandable.

In the classroom, as well, you identify yourself as "teacher." After all, you have a very well-defined role to play in the lives of your students. You are the authority, both in terms of who knows the subject matter and who is in charge.

In reality, though, despite the common ground shared by the thousands of teachers active in the educational field at any one time, "teacher" should not define you. You bring a unique blend of traits to the activity of teaching. There is not another teacher exactly like you, with your combination of background, personal and professional experience, temperament, personality, and relationships. When you walk into your classroom, you are much more than "teacher." You are you.

If you teach in an abstract or by-the-book way, while eliminating what is unique about your style and personality, you will suffer all kinds of needless frustration and conflict. You will also rob your students of some of the richest experiences that they are likely to have under your tutelage. It is when you invest your subject matter with what makes you unique that you bring the material alive for the people that you teach. It is when you let them see how you have personally understood and interacted with your material that they begin to understand the process of learning. And it's when you allow your true self to teach, in all its changing and growing ways, that you and your students have the opportunity to learn together.

Consider your own history with the teachers from whom you have learned. Which ones do you remember best? Who enriched your experience the most or had the greatest positive impact? Ask yourself this question: Was it what they did or who they were that made them so important to you as their student?

2.

Be the Authority

There was a time when teachers universally dressed in formal clothing, arranged their classrooms in rank and file, and conducted their classes as virtual dictatorships, however benign. The teachers ruled—at least in the classroom—usually with the full and unqualified backing of administrators and parents. The students either submitted or faced the prospect of discipline.

For better and worse, times have changed. Many schools have abandoned dress codes for students and teachers alike. Knowledge of past abuses and the fear of lawsuits have led many schools to forbid many of the punishments for rule-breaking that used to be standard. A media-soaked culture that glorifies rebellious and insubordinate behavior has led to a much greater tolerance of verbal disrespect among students and teachers. And traditional classrooms have given way, in many instances, to learning centers, unconventional seating arrangements, and "open classrooms."

Some of these changes reflect a productive rejection of rigidity in education. They recognize that students have many different learning styles and speeds, and learn best when they participate actively in and out of the classroom. Other changes, however, have blurred the boundaries between teacher and student, and adult and child.

There are some boundaries that actually promote an atmosphere conducive to learning. They encourage respect between teacher and student, as well as student and student. Some boundaries help establish a teacher as both the person in charge and the person with expertise. Students can expect a teacher to be the person that they can look to for accurate information and feedback, as well as for a safe and stimulating learning environment.

More than ever before, it is up to you, the teacher, to set the boundaries and exemplify the behavior that demonstrates your authority and expectations in the classroom. Your students come from a variety of backgrounds and bring with them many different ideas and value systems. You need to tell them what's what when they're in your classroom. Establish your authority at the outset, and demonstrate your authority over time. Your students will respond accordingly with respect and attention.

3.

Be Consistent

Nothing is more disconcerting to a student than a teacher who keeps changing "the rules." When a teacher fails to communicate expectations clearly or follow through with promises or consequences, the student's ability to succeed is compromised.

You can serve your students' best interests by first deciding for yourself what you expect of them and yourself. Many schools have standard ways of helping their teachers set academic goals and spell out basic parameters for student behavior. But what an institution mandates in general and how a teacher accomplishes it with his or her specific students are two different things. You need to decide and keep track of the particular expectations that you will communicate to your students.

Depending on the complexity of your teaching situation, you may find that sheer memory is not sufficient for either you or your students. Putting in writing what you expect, what penalties will be applied when students do not comply, and what rewards will be given when they do is a great way to lay solid ground under your teaching.

Once you've established expectations, it's extremely important that you follow through. Presumably, by thinking out what you expect ahead of time, you have established a fair and helpful set of guidelines. Holding your students to the standards that you've created is a big part of their learning process. Remember, though, that this isn't applicable only to your students. If you promise to grade papers by the end of each week, for example, make sure that you do it. You will build your students' trust and model the consistency of performance that you want to see your students achieve.

It happens, of course, that we sometimes create unrealistic expectations that lead to failure and frustration for our students or ourselves. If you discover that you're asking too much of your students, it's okay to make changes. You can communicate these changes in a way that is as instructive to your students as the material they are learning.

Whatever you hope or expect, be clear about it with your students. Hold yourself to the same standards of fulfillment that you expect from them. Keep it simple and straightforward, and you'll do everyone a big favor.

4.

Establish Boundaries

What's okay in the classroom and what's not? That's a question you need to ask yourself and communicate to your students if you're going to successfully create an atmosphere of mutual respect, trust, and safety. Often, a student's success in the classroom depends on knowing and understanding the boundaries. Your failure to set and enforce boundaries can be a direct path to your students' failure to learn and grow under your guidance.

The line between okay and not okay can be a fine one. You can explain and demonstrate the boundaries you set for your students. For example, you may want to make open discussion a part of your teaching. It can be an effective way of challenging students to think and respond to controversial ideas or opposing viewpoints. But unless you set down basic guidelines for courtesy and respect, you may very quickly find that your class discussion gets out of control. The simplest rules—let someone finish speaking before you begin; avoid personal attacks on the views and comments of others; let four other students speak before you speak a second time; and so on—not only keep your group discussion under control, but also elevate the conversation to civilized discourse and teach some valuable life skills.

You may like to promote an atmosphere of camaraderie and fun among your students, but even the most innocent fun can sometimes hurt feelings. Some humor is fine. Teasing is not. Laughter is good medicine. Laughing at someone or their mistakes is not. You can distinguish between good fun and hurtful joking with kindness and patience—but you cannot tolerate the latter. Establishing such a boundary means that every one of your students can enjoy a place of respect and appreciation in your classroom.

Depending on the age and background of your students, you may also need to set basic boundaries that have to do with physical contact, language, or personal property. Never be afraid to act as lawmaker in your own classroom. You have the right and the responsibility to tell them what will fly within that setting. In doing so, you may be responsible for teaching your students some of their most important lessons.

5.

Be Aware of Learning Styles

People learn in many different ways. Some are primarily visual in the way that they take in information. Others are more auditory or kinesthetic. Some people learn best from trial and error. Others learn by rote. Virtually all students learn best when they are actively involved in the material that they are being taught, but no one method successfully brings this about for all students.

Getting to know your students is crucial to understanding their individual learning styles. When you teach a class, you're dealing with the dynamic of the whole group, as well as attempting to relate to individuals. You need to watch students carefully for what gets them excited, in terms of subject matter and teaching method. You need to take note of when they struggle or fail. Over time, you'll begin to discern learning patterns in each of your students that can allow you to enhance their learning experience.

Obviously, the only way that you can pick up on the different learning styles of your students is to vary your way of presenting your material. Some people will respond to hands-on projects or out-of-class research. Some will soak up a straight lecture like dry sponges. Others will be at their best when they're given a chance to dramatize what they are learning. Whatever their styles, your students will be stimulated by variety. So will you.

It's tempting to stick with what you're used to. It often seems easier and safer to do the same old thing, rather than venture into new teaching methods or develop alternative lesson plans. But ease and safety will backfire, for both you and your students, because they inevitably lead to boredom and staleness—and teacher burnout. Work with variety to identify what turns your students on to learning, and then build that knowledge into the way that you teach. You'll not only be a more effective teacher, you'll have a lot more fun.

6.

Seek Expert Advice

In large part, teachers are expected to handle the challenges and trials of the classroom on their own. In addition to the academic demands of your job, classroom management and discipline fall primarily to you. So does relating to the administration that you answer to and the families of the children that you teach. You are also responsible for creating a positive learning environment. Your training probably prepared you for some of these responsibilities better than for others. The question is, what do you do when you run into a problem for which you don't have adequate experience?

Any number of factors can tempt us to carry burdens alone that would be better shared. One of the surest signs of your competence and professionalism will be your ability to judge when a challenge requires expertise or authority that you simply do not possess. It is a crucial part of your work as a teacher to understand the point at which you need to seek expert help and advice.

There may be occasions when it takes time to judge. In such cases, it is probably wise to confide in someone official while you assess the situation. Not only does this give you another person's judgment on the matter. It also puts someone else in the know, should a crisis of some kind develop.

Certainly, when you find yourself faced with emotional instability or dangerous behaviors in either your students or their families, your best course of action is to refer the situation to appropriate leaders in the school system, and if necessary, to external authorities. Your privileged relationship with a student may mean that you are one of the first to identify a problem, but it's not up to you to fix it.

Your students' challenges related to learning and social interaction fall within your purview. But here, too, you don't have to carry the burden alone. Make sure that you know what help and services are available through the school system. Apprise yourself of special programs offered throughout the school year. Take advantage of specialists in your school and town. At its best, education is a community activity. You don't need to be a solo performer, and you will find greater joy and satisfaction in your work when you let "the team" work with you.

7.

Know Your Limits

Professional limits have to do with your specific training, credentials, and experience. You've been officially equipped and certified in ways that define what your work can and should include. You have personal limits as well, however, and you are the only one who knows what these may be. They grow out of personal circumstances, energy level, past experiences, and other factors that are uniquely yours. No one will be able to tell you when you've reached these limits. It's up to you to recognize them and communicate clearly what they are when you are asked to violate them.

How can you identify reasonable limits for yourself? There are two ways to approach a personal assessment of your limits: one positive, and the other negative. On the positive side—that is, when you operate within your personal limits—work can be satisfying and energizing. Even when you are challenged, you feel confident of rising to the challenge in a timely, effective manner. You enjoy what you're doing more often than not. Your well of resources is deep enough to answer the demands of your duties and the needs of your students. You look forward to a new day.

By contrast, when you overstep your own limits, instead of being energized and encouraged by your work, you are drained by the demands of your job. You may find yourself short-tempered and unable to cope with everything calmly. You may experience feelings of anxiety or inadequacy, even in regard to responsibilities for which you have been trained and otherwise successfully handled. You may dread the beginning of your work week or the coming of a new day.

Be aware of your own stress signals, whatever they may be. Don't wait to run out of gas. As soon as you start showing signs of being stretched, take the time to reflect on what may be pushing you too far. Then take action to address the causes. If you're putting added strain on yourself with your personal choices, identify those choices and make appropriate changes. If the strain has come through decisions made by others, go to the ones responsible and talk it out.

Learning what your limits are will keep you and your students happier in the classroom. You cheat yourself and them when you let yourself be dragged into the overload zone.

8.

Take a Break

All formal teaching situations have breathers built into them. Whether they come in the form of personal days, holidays, sabbaticals, or leaves of absence, they are part of the package for good reason. Teaching demands the most of your abilities and energies. It requires ongoing training and up-to-date curriculum. Most of all, it depends on your good health and vitality. The breaks that punctuate a teaching schedule are intended to promote all of this.

A teacher's needs change throughout his or her career. What keeps you at the top of the game calls for more than one solution. Maybe your limitations in regard to technology are frustrating you. Perhaps you're physically exhausted. Your home life may be suffering from work-induced neglect. You may be feeling "stale" and disinterested in your subject matter.

You'll do yourself the biggest favor of your teaching life by approaching any potential time off with an awareness of your current needs. Sign up for an education-oriented computer course. Take a real vacation, leaving teaching completely behind for a bit, and regain some perspective. Take a week to give home your undivided attention. Sign up for a seminar that freshens your approach or adds to your knowledge. Or take yourself on an extended field trip that focuses on the subject that you teach. If you can afford it, you may even want to take a season off to regroup and rebuild your own intellectual interests.

The point is this: You are in a profession that recognizes more than most the need for "time out." Yet many teachers don't take advantage of the breaks available to them. As a result, they lose their enthusiasm and energy for what they are doing. When opportunities arise, make a point of using them. Take the time to plan ahead, and revitalize your teaching and your life.

9.

Share Your Interests

You know that there's a lot more to your students than what they study and produce in school. Other activities and interests add dimension to their personalities. The same is true of you—but do your students know that?

The extracurricular parts of your life make you well-rounded. They give you individuality and character. They also give you potential common ground and fresh learning hooks with your students. The books that you read, food that you eat, trips that you take, or games that you play can give your students positive ways to relate to you and your shared time in the classroom. However, you have to make yourself available in these ways in order for that to happen.

The way that you do this can be as simple as making it a point to mention your own preferences or activities at appropriate times in your classroom conversation. When you ask your students to share something about themselves or what they've done as part of a project or discussion, you can share, as well. If one of your students raises a subject that you have personal experience or interest in, you can communicate that. If someone brings up a subject that you've always wanted to know more about or be involved in, you can let them know that you'd like to hear more from them on the subject.

In addition, you may discover ways to use your own interests and experiences as an enriching part of your teaching. If you have a hobby or collection, you may want to incorporate it into a special unit or section of your classroom activity. If you've traveled to a destination that relates to your students or your subject matter, you can share your experience through photos, videos, and mementos. Your willingness to share in such a way may model for otherwise reticent students how to be more open in class.

You don't need to hide behind your "teacher" persona. In fact, you'll be a far more compelling teacher as your students understand how much more there is to you. They'll be better able to identify with you and imagine a grownup version of themselves. They may also be encouraged to venture into new interests themselves. Most of all, your ability to share with them will open doors to communication and growth that would otherwise remain closed.

10.

Reward Positive Behavior

The world offers plenty of feedback on what's wrong with our lives. News, gossip, and endless rules emphasize only negativity. That's why it's imperative that you, as teacher, find many ways to inspire and reinforce the positive in your students.

Keep in mind that when you are tired, distracted, or stressed, you tend to fall back on "default" reactions and behavior. So do your students. This makes advance planning for strategic handling of both positive and negative behavior imperative. Protocols exist on an administrative scale for how you can or should reward your students' successes and discipline their misbehavior. But what happens between you and your students in the classroom is far more organic than any set of rules.

Your personal dynamic with your class depends at times on your energy level and your temperament. It also depends to varying degrees on events and feelings that you and your students bring with you from outside of your class time. It can be affected by something as mundane as the weather or how a school team performed the day before. Unless you have worked through how to manage the ups and downs ahead of time, you are likely to react emotionally, and that often can focus your attention on the negative.

So how do you permanently shift the balance in your classroom from negative to positive? A starting point is to offer regular positive reinforcement of your students' honest academic efforts and good behavior. Find something encouraging to say about every contribution offered by one of your students, even if it's just, "That's an interesting idea. I'm glad you mentioned it. Who can add to that?" Make a point of assigning jobs to your students in the classroom, and remember to thank them for a job well done. Give verbal, as well as academic credit for extra work, including special projects, corrected assignments, and volunteer work. And extend the benefit of the doubt whenever it's in your power and good judgment to do so.

Think ahead about your responses to negative behavior, as well. Instead of immediately coming down on a student with anger or punishment, consider ways that you may be able to turn the situation into a teaching opportunity. Avoid humiliation in favor of discussion—in private, when it involves one or two only—and give students the chance to make reparations. When you help a student reason his or her way toward better behavior now, you're giving that student a valuable tool for a similar situation in the future.

11.

Establish the Mood

Sometimes you enter your classroom and sense immediately that there's something "in the air." The room seems to crackle with mischief or pent-up energy or distraction. Maybe you sigh inwardly and say to yourself, It's going to be one of those days.

Don't be too quick to let an unproductive atmosphere prevail. Whether or not you feel it, you are in charge while your students are with you. You can set the mood in your classroom by your actions and change the mood by your reactions. Like every challenge that you face in teaching, you can keep a negative atmosphere from taking over by consciously understanding the challenge and planning ahead for it.

Upcoming holidays, for example, can put a group of students into a state of excitement that makes it difficult for you to keep everyone on task. Perhaps during the few days before a break, you need to give the first ten minutes of class time to letting students talk about what's coming for them while they're out of school. Or you may find it helpful simply to acknowledge that everyone is getting pretty wound up. Promise them an early end to work time in exchange for their undivided attention at the beginning. Offer prizes, points, or special privileges for accomplishing the day's goals in good time and humor. You can take control of the mood and situation in your classroom by being on top of it from the start and taking steps to bring your students along.

Your good humor, patience, and firm attitude will go a long way toward setting the mood of your classroom. Remember that your students do more than act out their own issues and feelings. They react to you. If you're confident and supportive, they'll be more likely to follow your example.

12.

Model Respect

One of the most important attitudes that you can instill in your students, regardless of their ages, is respect—for you as the authority figure, for others as individuals, and for themselves as valued members of your class. Respect allows successful discipline, courteous class time, and individual growth. It lays the groundwork for an environment conducive to learning on all levels. It encourages academic success and good citizenship. With respect comes appreciation for boundaries.

Some students do not come from a home environment in which respect is the prevailing attitude. They haven't seen it in action from early childhood; they don't know what it means or what it looks like. You can talk about it, explaining that each person needs both to honor the rights and privileges of others and to be sensitive to the needs and feelings of others. But students must see signs of respect acted out for them. Until they observe your respect in action for every one of them, their families, other teachers, and the authority figures in your school, they'll be immune to the message.

Modeling respect means that you show your genuine care for the welfare, contributions, and feelings of every student, no matter how enjoyable or attractive you may find any particular individuals. Respect isn't about liking a person, and students need to see the truth of that. Modeling respect also means that you invest the time it takes to discover what is valuable in every person and exhibit your appreciation for what you find. It means that you go to the extra trouble of dealing with conflict or misbehavior in such a way that a student's intrinsic worth is upheld. Discipline focuses on learning better and doing better. Punishments should be no harsher than they have to be, and they should never preclude the chance for reparation and improvement.

Modeling and teaching respect take energy and conscious effort, but they pay enormous dividends in morale and motivation. When your students understand and experience how important they are to you, they will want to perform for you, and they will want to make you proud. You'll have the pleasure of drawing out the best in each of them.

13.

Be Flexible

While the importance of planning and routine cannot be denied, any experienced teacher knows that the best-laid plans often go awry. A fire drill sends everyone scuttling. A leak in the ceiling means moving desks or chairs. A big item in world news causes a distracting hubbub. Your students have something serious or exciting—but not academic—on their minds. Whatever the cause, class time sometimes simply refuses to go as you planned.

What can you do? For starters, get it planted firmly in your head that the unexpected will happen. Knowing and anticipating that life will dish out surprises can take some of the frustration out of unexpected change. You can choose to feel persecuted or subverted by the unexpected, or you can adopt the more realistic, philosophical stance that everyone has to deal with this.

Consider as well that sometimes a little shakeup in schedule actually promotes unusual, interesting teaching opportunities. Obviously, it's hard to plan ahead for the particular unexpected situation. However, you can certainly think creatively about what you might do when a class period is unexpectedly shortened, or when personal tragedy or national crisis hits. You can pay attention to the ways that other teachers make the most of surprises and tuck their tactics into your own bag of tricks.

You need to be a lifelong learner to teach. Let classroom surprises act as a tutorial in flexibility. Instead of being flustered, become focused. Be ready not only to roll with the punches, but to make use of them. Teach your students, through their experiences with you, that some of the best moments in life are the ones that we don't plan.

14.

Create Surprises

Once you've mastered the art of flexibility, you're likely to find the idea of surprises less alarming. That's the best time to start planning surprises in the classroom that keep your students alert and enthusiastic. They'll enjoy periodic wake-up calls and stimuli to keep them fresh and engaged.

Keep in mind that a pop quiz is not one of the more involving and enjoyable surprises that a student can face. It serves a motivational and instructional purpose, but it also causes a fair amount of dread. If you want to make the most of the element of surprise in your classroom, you'll need to put more creative effort into what you're doing than that.

When are your students most in need of a change of pace? That's a good time to plan something unexpected. After a big push to finish a project or complete an exam, you may want to introduce an activity that lets them play with the subject matter instead of working on it. Food in the classroom, games, music, a surprise guest (human or otherwise), a video that takes a nonacademic approach to classroom material—any of these can add texture and excitement to material that has begun to grow stale.

What do your students enjoy outside of your classroom? That's a great source of potential surprise for you to consider. Whether they are into sports, drama, music, shopping, computer games, or travel, your students will appreciate finding their interests brought into your classroom. You'll have to work out ahead of time what you want to do—but your students don't need to know until they arrive and meet the unexpected.

What resources are available to you through your teaching institution? Make sure that you know the answer to that question and give some serious consideration to how you can make the resources work for you. Be on the lookout for people, equipment, and materials that offer alternatives to the standard fare. Keep a file of good ideas that you run into in professional journals, in news reports, from colleagues, and through surprises of your own.

Knowing what you are looking for is a huge first step toward finding it. Let it be known that you want ideas for unusual ways to engage your students, and you're liable to find yourself with more than you have time to use. Your students won't be the only beneficiaries.

15.

Encourage Originality

Each of your students has something unique to offer. Such aspects of their experience and personality play a role in how they perform, especially when fulfilling assignments and requirements. It is unquestionably an essential part of a student's education to learn how to understand and fulfill what is required or requested in a given assignment. But a student also benefits from opportunities to shine in his or her own special ways.

There are parts of your curriculum that are flexible. You can encourage your students to think beyond the requirements of an assignment, to bring their special talents to the table. Maybe they have a creative, unorthodox way of completing an assignment. Perhaps they wish to express themselves in a medium seldom used in class. Students will surprise you when given the chance to showcase their interests and talents in a safe, respectful environment.

Most disciplines have developed and benefited from creative thinkers working "outside the box" to produce new ways of looking at a subject or expressing a truth. Creativity and originality are a vital part of self-expression, learning, and understanding. You may have students with brilliant potential who will never thrive while they are coloring inside the lines. They will thrive if you let them step outside convention and reinvent their work.

Look for ways to provide creative students with opportunities to exercise their originality. Encourage them to learn and follow traditions and rules by giving them some freedoms along the way. Your brightest student will not flourish if he or she is stifled and bored. However, if you acknowledge such a student's innate ability and pay it some respect, you'll discover new riches. In fact, you may discover that some of your "problem" students are actually the most gifted ones, who, lacking outlets for acceptable creativity, turn to mischief. Letting them shine in ways that come naturally to them will have the added benefit of making your job as teacher more engaging, as well.

16.

Don't Ask for What You Won't Do

When it comes to making assignments, a teacher needs to take a step back and reclaim some of the idealism and energy that made him or her want to go into teaching in the first place. Your students are worthy of meaningful work. They have no choice, if they're pre-college, about going to school. Many of them already have a difficult time seeing the point in much of what they're asked to do and learn. To give them dull or repetitive work or assign tasks that don't suit their learning style is to guarantee that they'll learn to hate school. In some cases, they may learn to hate the idea of learning—an attitude that can dog them for the rest of their lives.

Such attitudes can also occur when assignments are sent home over holidays and vacations. Some of these assignments may not be your choice. Your school may mandate a summer reading list or an exam schedule that bridges a break. That shouldn't keep you from carefully considering the impact of your assignments on the quality of your students' lives and good health. If you feel that a level of mandated work has surpassed what is reasonable or wise, go to bat for your students. Talk to administrators about other ways of achieving goals or finding productive compromises. Just as you get tired and anxious and need your breaks, so do your students. Look at assignments from their point of view, and consider how you'd feel about it if they could turn the tables on you.

Consider what you ask of your students in their everyday assignments. There are students for whom a spotlight assignment (giving a speech or making a solo presentation) is worse than torture. Think about whatever it is that gives you the most anxiety, and learn to have a heart. There's more than one way to accomplish what you want. You just need to identify your goal and find alternatives.

Obviously, this isn't to say that students should never be asked to stretch or grow. The stretching experiences are part of what promotes learning and broadens horizons. Assignments over vacation may help maintain hard-won study habits. But even with that in mind, you can take a proactively compassionate approach to what you ask of your students. They have the same needs for rest, meaning, and interest that you do.

17.

Foster Cooperation

It's a truism (for good reasons) that the best learners are doers. People who have to get their hands dirty within a learning environment take hold of their subjects far more effectively than those who are allowed to sit and have someone else do all of the work. A teacher who instructs this way makes his or her students active, lifelong learners.

Fostering cooperation in the learning process can be as easy as maintaining a routine of rotating classroom duties—such as cleaning the chalkboard, passing out papers, and changing the classroom display—and as complicated as assigning students small parts of the curriculum to present to their fellow students and you. As you get to know your students and their gifts and interests, you can find ways that involve them in tasks that appeal to their sense of who they are and what they do well. The question, "Who knows how to…?" can unearth talents and desires for recognition that you never guessed were there. A simple, "I've noticed how well you…" can give a student the confidence to go beyond the minimum effort in the classroom and get involved.

The emphasis on cooperation in the classroom helps students understand that learning is a joint effort. Teaching requires give and take: someone to impart wisdom, and another to exert an effort to absorb that information. A vital interaction exists when learning takes place, and when you foster a cooperative effort in any way in your classroom, you nurture that interaction.

Sometimes, it may seem less trouble to do the lion's share of the work in your classroom, but every experienced teacher knows that as students feel invested in their class and take responsibility for their part in it, they rise to higher levels of performance and retain more of what they learn. Remember what you know about the value of involving your students in the cooperative effort of learning, for their sakes and your own.

18.

Be a Student

It's impossible to talk about the teaching experience without coming back again and again to the mutual nature of the enterprise. Your students learn by taking in a set course of study with you at the helm. They also receive inspiration by watching as you engage yourself in the subject matter specifically, and in life generally. When you are enthusiastic and involved in what you are teaching, they are much more likely to be the same. When you display curiosity about your subject, they begin to catch on to what learning is really about—the desire to understand and connect with some aspect of the wide range of information and experience that comprise our human existence. When you display enthusiasm for your subjects, students can see possibilities for themselves.

Being a teacher who is also a student will almost certainly mean some form of continuing education in your field. Happily for the average teacher, educational institutions often support that effort, with both mandated requirements and creative opportunities—in some cases, even financial support. Take advantage of every opportunity to be the student. Take the courses and seminars. Even when the topics seem less than inspiring, attending workshops will give you the chance to interact with other teachers and test your ideas and perceptions against those of others. When you least expect it, you may stumble upon some valuable information or advice that speaks to a challenge that you haven't been able to meet.

Being a student, as well as a teacher, can also mean pursuing your personal interests and talents. They don't need to pertain directly to what and whom you teach. When you journey toward learning, you gain wisdom and perspective. You replenish your own stores of energy and hope. And your students will benefit from having an inspired teacher lead the way down the path of learning.

19.

Be Predictable

Predictability is a drawback, if you're talking about the ways in which you present subject matter. Teaching the same old way, year after year, becomes a dry, disappointing way to reach your students. People are, by nature, curious, creative, and able to take in information at a rate far faster than human speech. Any teacher who relentlessly follows the same format at the same pace with the same basic assignments and expectations will quickly face a group of very bored students. In other words, keeping the element of the unexpected in the presentation of subject matter is a plus.

In matters of discipline and social interaction, however, predictability is a must. The teacher who unexpectedly changes the rules of the classroom—who has fits of anger or shifts between teasing and berating, who demands student performance one day and shrugs it off the next—creates a level of insecurity and anxiety in his or her students that can only detract from the students' learning experience.

Every person needs a measure of stability. We like to know what is expected of us. We yearn to have a clear sense of what consequences will follow which actions. We may choose to get ourselves into a jam, but we really want to know ahead of time what we're choosing. The teacher who employs an arbitrary style of relating to students robs them of an emotional foundation from which to act, react, learn, and grow.

Know who you are and what you expect from your students. Let them in on the secret of your personal "rules." Then stick to them. Your students will be happier, more secure, and eventually, more accountable for what they do.

20.

Accept Differences

The variety of personalities, appearances, backgrounds, and learning styles among your students is part of what can make your classroom a rich and rewarding environment. The same variety among your colleagues and administrators can bring a wonderful mix of talents and interests to your teaching experience. The differences among human beings can be fascinating and energizing.

Sometimes, however, differences between you and others, whether they are your students or your professional peers, turn out to be less than engaging. In fact, they can be annoying, confusing, or mystifying. You want others to understand and appreciate you, and you want to be able to relate to them in an effective way, but occasionally your differences can make such interaction a Herculean task.

You can save yourself angst by distinguishing between differences that can and should be resolved—opinions, ideas, arguments, goals— and those that cannot. Differences of personality, style, or culture often defy total resolution. They demand that you seek to understand, accept, and even embrace. They require that you see beyond them to the common ground that you share with another person.

The more you come to accept differences in the teaching environment, the more you can learn to make the most of those differences. You can learn new ways of seeing and understanding through the eyes of another person. You can draw on the resources those who have different backgrounds can impart. Someone from a foreign land may have interesting stories to tell of an unfamiliar place and culture. Someone with a different family or religious background may have traditions and customs that can make for exciting in-class exchanges. And someone who has experienced the phenomenon of being the "outsider" can offer new insights and teach compassion to those who have only known the life of the "insider."

Take the time and effort needed to face differences squarely and deal with them creatively. In a diverse culture, the more understanding you can foster in those around you, the better. You can play a significant part in nurturing new and stronger bonds among people who might otherwise turn their differences into impermeable walls of prejudice and animosity.

21.

Know Your Students'
Non-Classroom Lives

When students enter your classroom, whatever their ages, they do not arrive as the proverbial *tabula rasa*—the clean slate. Their experience with you may figure largely in the landscape of their lives, or you may be a mere blip on their screen. But you can be sure that all of their experiences previous to this one will have had an impact on them. Family concerns, friendships, fears, joys, insecurities, and triumphs are all encrypted on their brains by the time that your students enter your domain.

If you want to know how to reach your students, you need to take all of the facets of their lives into account. You need to be able to say, "Remember when you…?" or "Think about how it feels when you…" As you find connecting points between your students' lives and your subject matter, you help them learn and to take part in their education. They'll come to see that learning has relevance to who they are and where they come from.

Obviously, there will be much that you never know about your students' extracurricular activities, but don't let that keep you from seeking to understand some part of what they experience outside of class. Make a point of knowing what sort of family they come from, how many siblings they have, and where they fall in the age lineup. Discover, if you can, what they look forward to, how they spend leisure hours, and what they believe.

It's also helpful to understand your students' fears. Do they walk out of (or into) your classroom with confidence and a sense of safety, or do they carry a feeling of dread within them. Some of their fears will have an immediate impact on their performance in school. If their home or neighborhood feels threatening, they may literally be too scared and preoccupied to concentrate on homework. If they have been teased by friends about good grades, they may want to appear disinterested and "cool" by hiding their academic ability in the classroom. They may fear failure and panic when they have to take exams.

Much of the behavior that you encounter in your classroom will have its source in something or someone outside of class. When you become friendlier with your students and take an interest in them as individuals, you'll pick up clues about what makes them tick. With this valuable information, you stand a much better chance of helping them find success in your classroom. The benefit for you is a group of students who feel understood and cared for.

22.

Acknowledge Special Days

Special days come in a wide variety of packages. Some are recognized school vacation days that offer a change of pace and place. There are other occasions that can bring you some refreshment and fun, as well, especially when you make a point of finding ways to bring them into your classroom. Whether you give a half hour to celebrating or use the occasion to tailor your curriculum in a novel way, you can make special days one of your tools for energizing your teaching.

Make a point of remembering every student's birthday. If you're dealing with younger children, they may contribute goodies from home. But you don't have to depend on that, nor do you have to leave older students (including adults!) out. Everyone likes to be honored once in a while. Find inexpensive ways of highlighting the birthday of the moment—with a banner, dime-store favors, some lively music, or simple refreshments—and create traditions that students can look forward to. You'll want to provide for the students whose birthdays fall on non-school days or during vacations. It's a simple, meaningful way to make a day different and your students important.

Think about holidays that are not generally recognized by your school or by many of your students. Plenty of information is available on the customs and meanings of religious and national holidays not typically celebrated by the mainstream. If you have students who come from unusual backgrounds, you have a natural source of information and participation, and you can give them a chance to shine. Emphasizing such times, even without a direct connection to your curriculum, contributes to the understanding that the world can be a very small place.

Watch the news for national or local events that can be made meaningful in your classroom. Election days beg for some discussion, even mock elections and speeches. The launch of a space shuttle, the christening of a new ship, the unveiling of a much-awaited book, or the start of a new sports season can afford you opportunities to make an adventure out of your usual lesson plan. These breaks in routine will create a sense of enjoyment for both you and your students. Your classroom will be a place of excitement and energy.

23.

Earn Your Students' Trust

Trust is essential to effective teaching. Trust promotes effective communication, self-confidence, determination, and the ability to delay gratification. With trust, you can be your students' guide and mentor, their advocate and advisor. Trust allows you and your students to engage in the learning process as a team.

The ingredients of trust are not all that mysterious, although they can slip away from you in the midst of weariness, frustration, or demoralization. Trust grows out of integrity. When you show yourself to be honest and true to your commitments and your principles, your students have a basis for putting their trust in you. Courtesy and consistent kindness will cement that trust.

There are many ways for you to demonstrate your integrity. When you try to understand your students as individuals, you show them your intention to treat them with respect and fairness. When you take the time to express what you expect of yourself, as well as of them, and then follow through consistently, you earn credibility.

When you give attention to your students' needs, you show that you can be depended on to listen and respond. And when you never fail to deliver an apology for a mistake or misunderstanding, you prove that you can be counted on in the long run, no matter what rough spots appear along the way.

The bottom line on trust is this: When you have it, you hold the key to effective teaching in the palm of your hand. Your teaching becomes grounded in the relationships that you develop with your students, allowing technique to play a supporting role.

Earn trust. Protect it with compassion. The positive impact on your students will be immeasurable.

24.

Vary Your Approach

Variety counts when you are presenting even the most standardized and prosaic of subject material. Whether a student is an ace in the academic arena or struggles with learning differences, he or she will benefit from the stimulation that variety offers. At its simplest, varying your teaching approach staves off boredom (both your students' and yours) that gets in the way of so many students' success in the classroom.

More important, variety of approach increases the odds that you will meet more of the learning needs of your students. What speaks to one may be quite different from what turns the light on for another. It's not just a matter of I.Q.; it has to do with what students have been exposed to and what they enjoy. A student who grew up on an active commercial farm starts at a very different place from one who grew up in New York City. An athletic kid may have a different take on a subject than an artistic type or a student whose ears perk up when the discussion turns scientific.

Varying approach in your lesson plans is only one aspect of variety in your classroom. Try changing the environment in which your students learn. Change the seating arrangement. Orient the class in different ways, so that you don't always make your presentations from the same spot in the room or sit in the same place when they are working without you. It's amazing how even a subtle change in the ordinary arrangement of things can rekindle interest and energy.

It's important to remember that you may have to vary your personal approach to particular students. You may run into surprising responses from one or another student and be at a loss to account for it. Unless you try a different tack, you may never break down the barrier that you sense. Offer your help in a different way. Students will likely be surprised and encouraged by your willingness to try again and again.

It has been said that variety is the spice of life. Season your classroom liberally with it. You'll find that you've added flavor for everyone including yourself.

25.

Accept Moods

There is no way that your classroom can remain unaffected by moods. Whether you're the moody one, you have one or more students on a high or in a funk, or the whole atmosphere seems infused with a particular temper, your class will feel its influence. You can't avoid moods or the power that they often exert, so your best bet is to learn how to recognize, accept, and deal with them.

You'll probably know if you're the "carrier" when a mood seems to grip your class. You know your own moods well, and you may have long since learned what you need to break out of them. If so, make it a point to do what you need to do before you have to interact with your students. It may be as simple as taking a moment to catch your breath and self-consciously adjust your attitude. Maybe you remind yourself why you teach and whom you intend to benefit. Moods can be self-centered. Concentrating on someone other than yourself can free you, at least for the length of a class. If you find that nothing will shake a bad mood, you can do your students a favor by warning them that this is not going to be one of your best. Even confessing to how you are feeling can sometimes take the edge off.

You won't be the only one to enter your class in a mood, however. You have much less control over the moodiness of your individual students. Depending on the person, you can choose to privately address the mood, asking whether there's something you need to know or can help with. If it's disruptive to the class as a whole, you can acknowledge the mood, while insisting that the distracting behavior stop. A conversation after class may help you get to the bottom of it.

Some moods, however, defy explanation and can't be changed. Your best course of action is to ride them out with the sufferer. Let Jane remain uncharacteristically quiet. Let Joe stare out the window while he works his mood through in his own way. Have some patience. If, on the other hand, you see that a student has undergone a long, lasting mood change in a negative direction, you may want or need to look further. Children suffer from clinical depression the same as adults, and when they do, they need the same medical and psychological assistance.

Accept that moods exist. Look for what brings them on and seek to soften them when they have a negative effect on your teaching. Most of all, remember the age-old wisdom: "This, too, shall pass."

26.

Respect Privacy

By and large, your relationship with your students has very real and well-defined limits. You have an area or age-level of expertise, and your job requires that you use that knowledge to inform and encourage the growth and learning of your students. In other words, your relationship is a professional one and needs to be treated as such.

Clearly, experienced teachers know that their students' personal lives sometimes intrude on their ability to do their job in an effective manner. To some extent, unless you know and understand what goes on outside the classroom, your ability to teach will be diminished. It is often possible through writing assignments, in-class discussions, and after-class friendliness to pick up enough of a notion of who and what your students are for you to do your job as well as possible.

There will be instances when you receive only hints of what may lie beneath the surface appearance and behavior of a given student. It can be difficult to discern the difference between what needs to be addressed and what falls into the category of "private." This is all the more true because we live in an age and culture in which the idea of personal privacy is taking a hit. The media oversteps the bounds of privacy for the sake of headlines or sound bytes. The "tell-all" mentality of our culture has transformed into a general disregard for people's private lives. Tragic public events have led us to understand the risks of too much privacy in the public sector. You may sincerely wonder at times how to juggle your professionalism with your duty to protect and provide for your students.

Keeping your professional relationship with your students firmly in mind may help you maintain an active respect for their privacy. When in doubt about whether to step over the line, seek out someone whose judgment and knowledge you respect. Look for advice both inside and outside of your own institution and keep the matter utterly confidential until you have a firm idea of what you should do. Once breached, a student's privacy can be hard or impossible to restore.

27.

Be a Talent Scout

Nearly every individual, given the opportunity, has some area in which he or she can shine. The big talents can be relatively easy to spot. A person who has a gift for music, art, public speaking, or gymnastics tends to find the spotlight. Academic talent tends to be recognized. In both instances, students get encouraging feedback and opportunities to develop.

It is one of the well-recognized ironies of traditional education that some of the most imaginative students express their talents in ways that are neither recognized nor rewarded by mainstream measures. It falls to the individual teacher—you—to spot and encourage such students in their unconventional abilities. These are the students who doodle in the margins, surprise you with unexpected connections in class discussion, or seem to be picking daisies when you have a straightforward assignment in the works. It's worth the effort to tune in to these students. If such abilities can be coaxed into action, the results can be rich, both for the individual and the group.

Some students, however, define "normal." They don't excel academically or artistically. They don't tend to dream big dreams or draw positive attention to themselves. These students, perhaps more than any others, need your help in identifying ways in which they can make a special contribution and exercise their individual strengths. For these students, you need to redefine your ideas of "success." Consider such positive contributions as friendliness, energy, physical strength, listening ability, organization skills, persistence, trustworthiness, or everyday courage. In the world at large, any of these qualities plays a valuable, even crucial role, yet they rarely receive the credit or encouragement that more obvious talents do.

Pay attention to the gifts, skills, and characteristics of your students that are waiting to be nurtured. If you can allow them expressions in your classroom, by all means, do so. If you see a hidden gift that could use some outside reinforcement, you may want to check out ways that your learning institution might help. If you're teaching youngsters, make a note of what you observe in the notes that go home to parents. Not all parents are tuned in to what is special about their own children, especially if it falls outside of the traditional arenas. You may be in a position to give parents, the larger community, and even the student him- or herself a new vision of that individual.

28.

Delegate

People tend to be most enthusiastic and involved in enterprises in which they feel that they have a personal investment. Your students are no different. Giving them a sense of ownership in your class will exert a powerful influence on their performance and attitude. They will feel such ownership when they are given real responsibilities, the resources to fulfill those responsibilities, and recognition for their successes.

What needs to be done in your classroom? Do you have chalkboards that need to be cleaned, bulletin boards that need to be designed, or weekly assignment sheets that need to be handed out? If you have younger students, do you need the calendar to be changed, the snacks handed out, books put away in the right place, attendance sheets handed in, or the line headed up? If you have older students, is there extra research that would enhance your material, information about department events that would involve your students, or an informal data sheet that needs producing?

All manner of jobs and responsibilities exist in a learning environment. Few, if any, have to fall to the teacher alone. The more ways that you discover to share the workload and delegate tasks to your students, the more involved and important they are likely to feel and behave. Granted, if such delegation doesn't come automatically or easily to you, it will feel like more work than it's worth, at first. You may also feel a loss of control. Don't let that stop you! Over time, it is no more work to hand over jobs than to do them. As far as the control of your class is concerned, the more you lead your students into taking and fulfilling responsibilities, the more they'll learn to control themselves and contribute positively to the community.

29.

Let Your Students Teach

There are several ways of enabling students to act as teachers in the learning environment. They can take your lesson plan and make a teaching presentation of it. They can turn things that they've learned outside your class into instructional presentations for you and their fellow students. They can act as mentors or tutors for students at their own or lower levels. In any of these cases, the value is the same. We learn most when we have to teach. We gain self-esteem and confidence when we take on leadership roles.

Most traditional learning institutions provide occasions for students to make oral or visual presentations before a group of their peers. Make the most of these assignments. If you have students who suffer from stage fright or very low self-esteem, give them all of the help that you can to diminish their fear. Perhaps you could first assign a group presentation, or give some coaching to individual presenters. You may also allow some flexibility of subject or presentation style, especially while you are still building esprit de corps among your students. Permitting a student to work with material and media that make him or her feel more competent can pave the way for greater challenges later.

You may find that there are also times when your students can contribute to your class time with presentations of their own material. If you have students who travel, you may be able to devise assignments that draw on their experiences and allow them to bring what they've learned into your class. If students take private lessons or go to special camps, they may have skills or information to share. Unusual cultural backgrounds often provide material for excellent presentation opportunities, as well.

Don't forget that some of your students learn at a faster rate than their peers. Those students can be of real help to slower learners. Depending on the age range and situation, you may also be able to hook your own students up as tutors with younger classes. Some schools have programs through which older students contribute a certain number of hours reading to young students or helping as aides in reading, writing, and arithmetic.

Whatever chance you can give your students to do the teaching, be sure to do so. They will not only better learn the material that they need to present, they will learn how to be better students in general.

30.

Major on the Major

There is virtually no end to the issues, problems, details, and dramas that demand your attention as a teacher. The job description for prospective teachers should routinely include the title "juggler," because you will certainly be called upon to balance any number of concerns at one time. This can sometimes make a teacher's life frustrating and overwhelming.

There's no cure for the complexity of a teacher's job. It's part of what makes it as challenging and rewarding as it often is. You can, however, develop ways of eliminating some of the stress. Simply put, you have to learn to distinguish what is important from what can wait and channel your efforts in the right direction.

In medicine, the common term for this principle is *triage*. Triage requires that you sort your demands according to how crucial they are, how quickly they must be handled, and how they stack up against competing demands. If you have a situation that daily jeopardizes the success of your entire class (a construction project with a jackhammer right outside your classroom during class time), that problem will rank higher for the allocation of immediate attention than an ongoing "wish list" item that has gone unmet (you've asked for six months to have the overhead projection screen fixed). In the long run, the latter may pay longer lasting benefits, but until the former is resolved, all bets are off.

All of us succumb to urgency from time to time. Sometimes, it is easier to answer the loudest, latest holler instead of prioritizing. Stick to a policy of triage. Don't let minor issues become your major stumbling blocks. Relegate your greatest strengths to what counts. Major on the major.

31.
Make the Most of Diversity

Growing awareness education has improved educators' perception of the need for greater attention to diversity in the classroom. Because of the broad range of ethnicity, language, and religion in the modern Western world, we can no longer assume that there is a homogeneous group of students in the classroom. Curricula have been updated to reflect a socioeconomic system that no longer assumes a male-dominated Caucasian society. Storybooks celebrate different races and cultures, without one sort of family experience treated as the norm. All of this is good, and whether your particular group of students represents the diversity celebrated in today's educational material or not, you and your students gain from the use of these materials.

In a class of students who come from similar backgrounds and socioeconomic groups, you may need to be creative in bringing diversity closer to their experience. All of the curricula in the world will not make the impact that firsthand exposure and experience provides. Invite representatives of diverse groups to come into your classroom to share their perspectives and experiences. You can also arrange exchange programs that give your students a face-to-face encounter with people their age whose lives and experiences are different from their own.

Of course, you may have a fair amount of diversity within the confines of your own group. If so, you should exploit this advantage in whatever way you can. Every positive message that you contribute to your students is a step toward greater tolerance among all human beings. Regardless of the tensions that exist outside of your classroom or region, you can create an atmosphere of trust and mutual aid that will inform our youngest citizens. Remember: Your own actions and attitudes will speak louder than any lesson plan. The more you show the way, the more your students will "get it."

32.

Create Anticipation

The writers who create our very popular television shows know the market value of a "cliffhanger" that keeps the audience in suspense from the end of one season to the beginning of the next. Novelists understand that to write a page-turner, they have to create a scenario in which the reader wants to stay invested in a story. Playwrights almost universally follow a pattern for dramatic action that creates enough tension in the progress of the story that the audience won't leave before the climactic final act. Even visual artists follow a design plan that creates enough visual interest to bring the viewer's eye back to the image again and again.

Suspense, or anticipation, is the key to creating and maintaining interest, and there's no reason why you shouldn't cash in on its value in your classroom. Your students need a reason to keep coming back to your teaching with enthusiasm and curiosity. If you have students who are easily bored, they need to take some ownership of their education. You can do that by requiring them to get involved in meaningful ways. It's your job to create momentum that moves your students along with you.

Look for hooks that help engage your students. Once you're into your subject matter, consider ways that you can end a class session by leaving open, intriguing questions on the table. Present your material, if possible, up to an exciting moment, and then postpone the next moment until your next class. Create mysteries about who may be coming to visit, what you have planned, or what the students will be doing themselves, so their curiosity is piqued. Develop a plan for room arrangement or display that doesn't happen all at once, but rather builds from one week to the next so that your students hurry in to see what's added. Consider engaging interest by trying some hide-and-seek with your material.

Learning can be as involving and stimulating as a great suspense story or beautiful piece of artwork. Put your effort into it, and you'll see a transformation in your classroom that will make other challenges a great deal simpler.

33.

Use Current Events

Teachers are always on the lookout for ways in which to make their lessons relevant to the lives and experiences of their students. Fortunately, or unfortunately, the world regularly provides material to which we can relate any field of study.

News-related applications of what you teach will be obvious, depending on your subject matter. For older students, you can easily create tie-ins that have to do with recent discoveries or events that may change or add to what is understood about your subject. You can examine current events in light of what has happened in the past or what might happen in the future. You can highlight the ways in which any world event calls on the resources and knowledge of humankind.

Young people, whether they know it or not, are on a constant hunt for role models and heroes. You can help inform that process by engaging them in learning about people's lives and activities in other places and circumstances. You can be a conduit for a larger, deeper perspective on the part that your students themselves will play in the world.

Don't miss this chance to enrich your lesson plans. To use current events, you need to keep yourself current. Subscribe to a good newspaper with national coverage, or take advantage of National Public Radio or one of the more substantive television offerings. Enlist the involvement of your students, as well, at whatever level is appropriate for them. If you find ways to make news hunting a part of your students' assignments, you will teach them to be more aware and responsible as members of the world community.

We sometimes get quite elaborate in our hunt for exciting additions to standard fare in the classroom. This one is easy. You only need to plug in and reap the rewards.

34.

Acknowledge Trauma

As a teacher, you can be sure that you will encounter the effects of traumatic incidents, not only in your own life, but also in those of your students, or in the world. Bad times can hit an individual or family at any time, and the effects of such circumstances will not stop at the door of your classroom. The death of a faculty member or student will affect the entire school population. A bus accident during a class trip, whether or not your students were directly involved, will produce more of a response. Events like an attack on or assassination of the nation's president or a much publicized terrorist event can shake the foundation of your students' feelings of well-being and safety.

It behooves you to think ahead to what you will do on behalf of your students in the event of grief or terror. The bad times are best survived and healed by the loving involvement of the larger community. If you are a classroom teacher, your students spend a lot of their time with you and others in the school. In large part, you are their community, and they rightfully look to you for accurate information, comfort, and safety. So what, specifically, do you do when disaster strikes?

First and foremost, acknowledge openly that people are suffering. There's nothing lonelier than unobserved grief. Sometimes, a simple statement, "I'm so sorry for what has happened," can ease the pain in some small part. At the same time, avoid platitudes. Comments such as, "Perhaps there was a good reason for this," or "Well, if she was sick and suffering, this is probably for the best," are cruel comfort. Likewise, don't let your own discomfort in the face of someone else's suffering tempt you to rush them through grief or confusion to a resolution. Deep, unhappy emotions take time to heal.

Remember, too, that most educational communities have some sort of "crisis team" ready to leap into action in the event of trauma. Make sure that you know what is available for you as faculty, and for your students. Professional training can be of inestimable help in hard times, and it's most unlikely that your institution expects you to know or do all that is needed without backup and support. Work as a team. The tough times won't disappear simply because you deal with them together, but people will grow, learn, and heal more readily when pain is met with the love and kindness of others. You can be the embodiment of such care in the lives of your students.

35.

Offer Alternatives

In social terms, assisting a student who can't seem to fit in with other students may be quite a challenge. If you teach in a large enough school, it's worth talking to other teachers about the student's problem and looking for clubs, class sections, or activities that might give him or her more congenial interaction. In a situation where few options exist, as in a special class with only one section, you may find that allowing the student to work directly with or for you offers that student the best social solution in the short term. Some students spend much of their school years out of sync with their peers. Identifying with their teacher, and feeling acceptance, can go a long way toward making students feel like they "fit in."

If your student has a conflict with you, it's up to you to address and resolve the problem. Be as honest with yourself as you can. Do you have a personality problem with the student? If so, you need to take responsibility for that and take whatever action is necessary to rise above your feelings. Seek help in understanding the student and where he or she is coming from. Often, when you know more about a problem person and put his or her difficult traits in the context of home and extracurricular life, you'll find sources for greater compassion. Talk through your own feelings with a confidant, and weigh them against the vital role that you play in the student's life. If the negative feelings seem to be coming solely from the student, make it a priority to get to the bottom of them. You may or may not be able to resolve the conflict, but you need to know its true nature. In rare cases, a teacher finds that personal conflicts with a particular student are serious enough that it is advisable to transfer the student to another section with a different teacher. Don't let pride or stubbornness prevent you from exploring all possible alternatives to letting such trouble get in the way of your student's learning.

Remember, too, that a student may not fit the mold of the educational approach that you take. Certainly, if you're teaching in a traditional school, you are obliged to demand that students meet the institution's fundamental standards. Some students will struggle. Use your position to evaluate why a student has trouble performing according to school standards. At the same time, make the most of opportunities to offer nontraditional ways for the student to learn and respond to material. If you can make inroads with a student who is having difficulty, you may be providing the bridge that will help him or her succeed over the long haul.

36.

Invite Special Guests

It's inevitable that listening to the same voice and seeing the same face across a desk or classroom, day after day, month after month, can have a deadening effect on students. The teacher becomes too familiar and predictable. The students pay less and less attention because they believe, rightly or wrongly, that they already know what to expect from their instructor. The learning process loses its excitement and vitality.

There's nothing like the infusion of new blood to perk up a tired class. Having any change can be productive in terms of waking the students (and teacher) up. It is all the better if the change includes a new face with a fresh perspective or a new way of approaching what the students are learning.

You know your subject matter. Every discipline has its fascinating little secrets and its share of intriguing experts, whether directly connected to the subject or involved in some ancillary aspect of it. By all means, look for the obvious connections and invite people who regularly make visits to schools or take part in seminars. People who practice their expertise in your region and have an interest in serving the community will probably be delighted to be asked, and will make a worthy contribution. Be on the lookout, as well, for local people with hobbies that pertain to your subject matter. Many amateurs who have an interest in local history, environmental issues, crafts, or collecting love to share their passion and often do so quite well.

Keep an eye on your local newspaper. Authors, celebrities, sports figures, and politicians may pass through your area. Curators of special exhibitions or performers of one kind or another are happy to fill out their itinerary while on the road. It never hurts to ask, no matter how notable the visitor. It is good public relations for them at the same time that it's a boost for you and your class.

37.

Add Nature to Your Environment

It doesn't matter what age group your students fall into—from preschoolers to senior citizens, students appreciate the presence of nature within the classroom. Whether you introduce green plants, flowers, arrangements of rocks or driftwood, a miniature fountain, or small animals, your classroom will be infused with a special dynamic.

The most obvious value of nature in your space comes from the beauty of it. While not all of your students may pay attention to the aesthetics of their surroundings, all human beings respond to beauty. When you make a point of adding natural touches to the place where you teach, you communicate respect for what you are doing and for the people who are on the receiving end. You say, without words, that you care enough to put your time and resources into your teaching environment. You care about your students and their sense of well-being.

For children, of course, projects in which they actually cultivate plants go beyond beauty. They see firsthand the mystery of nature's design as they plant seeds, tend them, and watch them sprout into life. They also see the results of neglect when they forget to water or feed their plants. This is also emphasized when caring for class pets. Students learn how important it is to fulfill commitments in a real-life situation with life-and-death consequences.

As we cultivate and appropriate nature within our spaces, we take on the role of nurturers. In a teaching situation, nature reinforces and embellishes what we're about. In return for our attention and appreciation, it offers beauty, instruction, and a sense of connection with the world around us.

38.

Look for Field Trips

Just as you seek to enhance your students' experience in the classroom with visitors and elements from the natural world, you can broaden their perspective with trips out of the classroom. The change of routine and environment will awaken your students' enthusiasm and curiosity.

Take advantage of any and all outings provided by the institution in which you teach. Make the most of programmed out-of-class events by preparing for them with your students. Talk about what's coming up and why you're doing it. Give students mini-assignments that don't require anything more than being observant and reporting on some aspect of what they see or do.

In addition, look for ways to get your students out of the classroom independent of school-sanctioned events. There may be natural tie-ins to your subject matter that can take them to a local art or natural history museum, zoo, botanical garden, or planetarium. Don't forget about your community's service and utility providers—

large community bookstores and libraries, town hall, the police department, the fire department, power plants, post offices, or animal shelters. With some cooperation, you can provide a fascinating look at some aspect of the way a community is run, drawing on the expertise of those who work in such places. At the same time, you can demonstrate the ways in which the skills and information that your students are gaining have been applied by people in the workforce.

Remember that a field trip can be as simple as a hike on a local nature trail or a scavenger hunt on the campus of the school itself. If it takes you and your students outside on a lovely day or gives you a chance to add physical activity to your students' schedule, you will have enriched their education. It has been said that it is not what you say or do to another person but rather the way that you make them feel that they remember long after. When you make learning exciting and organic, your students feel excited and positive.

39.

Rearrange Your Furniture

It's important for everyone, every so often, to stand on their head. It changes the force of gravity, makes you see things from a different perspective, and increases the flow of blood to your brain.

What happens when you rearrange the elements of the classroom to force a different perspective? The image is similar to the familiar, but it's also transformed, turned upside down, and distended. Your students may suddenly find that the people to whom they've become close no longer sit near enough for a passed note or a whispered comment. They have new individuals to observe and consider. In the process, they may also have new ideas and insights. And when you put yourself in a different spot in the room, they are forced to reconsider you. Like the furniture, you've become a little less predictable, a little more dynamic, because your physical relationship to them has changed.

There's much to learning and relating that we only guess at. However, stimulating observation skills and challenging students to relate in different ways can only build the effectiveness of the classroom experience.

40.

Create Challenges

M otivating students is arguably the greatest challenge a teacher faces. Unless a student gets personally involved, feels a desire to achieve, and exerts the effort required, the best efforts of a teacher accomplish little. Some of the feedback and evaluation built into traditional models of education—standardized testing, grades, and other results-based measures—are designed in part to provide motivation. Yet by their very nature, they risk discouraging as many students as they inspire.

This is not to say that grades and test scores have no place in motivating students. It is to say that the more diversified you can make the motivators, the more students you will touch. You don't have to depend on traditional measures to motivate your students. You can develop other sorts of challenges that will engage their interest in learning and growing.

What gets your students fired up? For competitive types, creating unofficial (ungraded) contests creates a desire to learn the "facts," achieve the next goal, or build the next skill. Create ways for students to compete against themselves, rather than their peers. Give them individually tailored benchmarks that allow them to see their goals and regularly measure their progress.

Look for ways to challenge your class as a whole or in smaller groups or teams. Keep track, for instance, of how many students solve an especially challenging problem or hand in a special assignment. Without naming names as the number grows, let it be known that the entire group will benefit in varying degrees depending upon how many fulfill the challenge. Don't make it all or nothing—there's almost always one or more students who won't comply, and you don't want those who do to get nothing for their efforts. Rather, make the rewards gradually more appealing, depending on the percentage of students who meet the challenge. Set a definite time frame, and follow through on what you promise. This is a method that works best when repeated, regardless of the content of the challenge. Over time, the students catch on to the pleasure and satisfaction of meeting a difficult goal and contributing to the group.

Overall, simply keep in mind that what motivates people comes in many forms. Look for what your individual students respond to. Is it praise? Rewards? Grades? Creating a tangible product? Taking a leadership role in a team effort? Making use of a specific strength? Once you know what gets them excited, you hold the key to firing them up.

41.

Define Success in Several Ways

Just as one source of motivation cannot energize all of your students, one definition of success cannot be applied to all—not if your primary goal is to help each student meet his or her full potential. A sense of having succeeded is crucial to the self-esteem of those students, regardless of their innate abilities. It falls to you to identify ways in which you can label every best effort a "success." You need to use every measure and personal observation that you have available to you to gauge the actual potential in each student.

The standardized measures available to you in an educational setting can certainly reveal a great deal, but do not depend on them alone. There's much to be learned from watching how students deal with others, how quickly they get a joke, how well they respond to challenges, and how well they communicate ideas outside of formal classroom situations.

Some students perennially underachieve, and you don't want to encourage such students to stop reaching. Neither, however, do you want to withhold earned kudos. A bright student who consistently hears how much better he or she could do can become just as discouraged as a less-bright student who never moves beyond average work. A student may lack the maturity to do better or have no sense of the importance of schoolwork and education. Or there may be some other impediment that you'll never know about. Regardless, you're more likely to see improved effort if you give positive feedback for good work than if you level criticism for goals not met.

With average students, you need to encourage their strongest efforts without expecting top-of-the-class performance. Make note of all of the ways that they show how hard they are trying, and never fail to praise successes. When correction is needed, make your comments constructive and informative. Give them opportunities to correct assignments, taking the time that they need to work it out. Remember that getting it right the first time is far less important than learning to persevere until a goal is successfully met.

The students who do get it immediately need positive feedback just as much as everyone else. If they seem unchallenged, let them work with students who could use some coaching. They will learn communication skills, as well as advance their own understanding of the material, as they try to help someone else.

Even while you look for academic successes in your students' lives, watch for success in how they relate to others, how they listen, and how they resolve conflict or share their talents. Think creatively about what success really is, and make sure you give it its due in the lives of your students.

42.

Be a Coach

Generally speaking, all coaches aim for the same results. Whether they focus on people in sports, the arts, or business, they work to take nascent ability and hone it until it is as sharp and effective as it can be. The best coaches share a number of traits that make the people they coach winners again and again.

Great coaches are ace evaluators. They observe the individuals that they coach in order to glean as accurate a picture as possible of what they can accomplish. Good coaches never knowingly set an individual up for failure by asking the impossible, nor do they settle for a mediocre performance when better is possible.

Good coaches recognize that an individual's fears, ego, dreams, disappointments, and accomplishments all play a part in what that person is ready or able to do. When the individual is impeded, they seek to understand and address the problem.

Coaches respect the individual. A great coach knows to put aside any hidden biases or preconceptions, and discover what is unique and valuable in each person. At the same time, successful coaches deal with individuals in the context of the larger group, whether it's a team, an ensemble, or a collection of independent contenders in a field of endeavor. We are all influenced by the performances around us. Coaches understand that their pupils must learn to deal with this aspect of life in order to succeed.

For this reason, coaches are careful to build on the strengths of the individual. People do their best, individually and in relation to others, when they respect their own abilities and learn to emphasize their best qualities. Many times, it takes a coach to recognize and encourage such qualities.

Inevitably, coaches face failures with their students. Good coaches treat a defeat as a learning opportunity. They encourage their charges to do more preparatory work, to try again, or to try in a different way.

Most of all, great coaches understand that the only real defeat is to give up. Great coaches don't give up on the people that they train. They coax, they instruct, they insist, and they demand—all in the context of knowing and honoring the individual.

No one is better placed to be a great coach than a teacher. Let the winning qualities of great coaches remain a part of your teaching and your students will be the winners.

43.

Be a Friend

A fundamental distinction characterizes a friend from a foe. A friend suffers with you, not from you. When you hurt, a friend hurts alongside you. When you lack, a friend is the first to notice and look for ways that the need can be answered. When you're a pain in the neck, a friend exercises patience, looks for hidden causes, and gives you the benefit of the doubt. On the other hand, when you laugh, a friend gets the joke. When you throw a parade, a friend never rains on it. And when you succeed, a friend throws the party to celebrate.

As a teacher, you have a professional relationship with your students that requires appropriate boundaries and distinctions. You can't be a buddy or a best friend in the typical sense and at the same time maintain the authority and objectivity necessary to do your job responsibly. You can, however, exercise the best qualities of a true friend: kindness, support, generosity, compassion, trustworthiness, and appreciation. Such responses to your students—to their successes and failures, joys and sorrows—in no way compromises the fulfillment of your mandate as teacher. Rather, it makes you a more convincing ally and brings out the very best in those that you teach.

Sometimes, in the throes of frustration, teachers vent with one another by making their difficult students the enemy. While this usually happens in private and is often done with tongue in cheek, it still has its effect. Don't demonize your students. They're people just like you, with the same needs for affirmation and understanding, and the same capacity to be hurt behind a mask of surliness, sassiness, or boredom. Ask any parents what they want from their child's teacher, and most will put "kindness" at the top of the list. That doesn't mean that they want you to overlook bad behavior or neglected schoolwork. They simply want you to remember that there's a fragile ego living inside that child. It's yours to wound or protect.

44.

Be an Advocate

Advocacy serves a valuable role in human society. For those in a position of relative weakness or powerlessness, being heard, understood, and considered can sometimes be an uphill battle, at best. In many cases, students are in just such a relationship with the institution in which they receive their education. While the administrators and directing boards ostensibly have the students' welfare and best interests at heart, they are removed from close interaction with individual students. Competing demands may turn their attention to less important matters.

As a teacher, you know your students as well or better than any other person in the educational system. You see firsthand how policies and protocols affect individual students or groups of students. You are the one most likely to observe special needs, troubling signs, and problematic trends. You are also the one who has the power and obligation to address such concerns to your institution's administrators. If you don't go to bat for your students, it's possible that no one will. If you don't lend your support to students' parents looking for help or change, it's possible that they won't get a fair hearing. And if you don't stand beside your students when they seek to voice their concerns directly to the powers that be, you may very well teach them to disrespect some of the most powerful rights that people living in a free society enjoy.

A teacher's single highest concern should be what's best for his or her students. Demonstrate your calling to your students by your actions. Be the one that they can rely on to put their interests at the top of the school's priority list. Be their voice when no one will listen otherwise. And stand their ground with them when they need support for their best interests to be served.

45.

Make Your Students
Your First Priority

Researchers have noted that one of the greatest stress-producers in a person's life is the habit of multitasking. This doesn't mean sharpening a pencil while keeping your eye on a rambunctious student. It means sharpening your pencil, watching the rambunctious student, thinking through what you're going to say in the faculty meeting, and listening to another student's questions, all at the same time. No one item on the list gets quality attention from you, with the possible exception of the pencil. You are too busy jumping from one to another to accurately track what one kid is doing and why, adequately plan your presentation, or take in what the other student's question is really about.

It's certainly unrealistic to suppose that you can give your full and undivided attention to only one thing all of the time. Yet, if you are going to give your students their due, you have to learn how to put the most important part of the job ahead of all other concerns during classroom hours.

The first step to putting first things first is awareness. Recognize the ways that you allow yourself to be distracted from your students during "their" time. Note the moments when your stress level rises or your attention wanders, and make a list of what the distracting elements are. Identifying those elements will help you strategize about ways to put them in their place.

Once you have a sense of the things that push you into heavy multitasking at your students' expense, spend some non-classroom time considering how you can manage the distractions. You may need to keep a notebook handy to record items that you will have to attend to later. Writing them down relieves you of the necessity of keeping them on your mind. You may also find it helpful to talk to other teachers. Share your experiences and your solutions for keeping your students as the top priority while at work.

You may find that when you build more focus into your school time, you'll take less of it away with you, freeing yourself at home and elsewhere to take quality care of other concerns. In turn, of course, this means that you'll have fewer concerns that travel with you into the classroom. Creative problem-solving in a quiet moment can save you endless hours of frustration and give back quality moments with your students.

46.

Look for What You Can Love

Teachers are people, and they experience the full range of human emotion in the classroom, just as surely as they experience it in their private lives. With the best intentions, they relate to some students more easily than to others, enjoy some students more, and just plain like some students better. Such gut reactions relate to students' habits, temperament, personality, and attitudes, and there isn't a whole lot a teacher can do about them.

Feelings, in and of themselves, are not right or wrong. They simply are. It's what we choose to do with or about them that moves us into moral or ethical arenas. We can't control immediate visceral reactions, but we can control what we think, say, and do as a result.

So what do you do about the student for whom your involuntary responses are more negative than positive? The first step is to acknowledge what you feel to yourself. Unless you can admit that you are put off by a student, you cannot take the next important step of figuring out what it is about the student that causes you to react in such a way. It may be that the student misbehaves, clings, whines, lies, or distracts others. Or you may be reacting to a personality conflict, a perceived lack of respect, dislike for the student's parents, or your own buried prejudices. Whatever the negative feelings, you need to name them and find their roots as honestly as you can.

Once you've named what's going on inside you, you have a good shot at doing something about it. You are no longer trapped by negative emotions. Stepping back from raw feeling allows you to apply principles and strategies that bring your responses back in line with your goals and beliefs. In turn, you are able to do the job that you signed up to do—put your students' best educational interests first.

Keep in mind that no student is one thing. Every person is a complicated mix of many characteristics and qualities. Dealing with your own negative feelings may involve internal work on your part that has little or nothing to do with the student. But work, as well, to find what you can love in that person—whether it is the quiet traits that take some searching out, the student's unrealized potential, or simply the student's intrinsic value as a fellow being. When you focus on what is worthy in a student that you have trouble with, you will have taken a giant step toward becoming a more compassionate, responsible, and effective teacher to all of your students.

47.

Demand Respect

Before you get up on your high horse about the apparent lack of respect in today's students, understand this: Respect is encouraged in students by the examples that they encounter at home, in school, and in the community. You can have an impact on the home and community environments that your students are exposed to, but it will have its limits. You do, however, play a pivotal role in the atmosphere that they encounter in your classroom and school.

Pay attention to your attitude toward national and local political leaders, administrators in your school, and other teachers. Your students will observe and internalize any negativity or lack of respect that you display. If you voice your opinions, however positive or negative, with an eye to preserving the dignity of the office held by someone, or upholding the intrinsic value of the individual, your students will see respect in action and begin to understand what it's about.

Consider, as well, the attitude that you communicate toward your students themselves. Respect begets respect. If you subject a student to sarcasm, public criticism, humiliation, or even teasing, you shouldn't be surprised to see him or her responding to you or others with similar behavior. If, however, you maintain fair and consistent standards, act with courtesy and cooperation, and remain relentlessly professional in your behavior, you'll show your students not only what you believe but also what you expect. What you do has far greater power to teach than what you say.

Finally, make a point of drawing students' attention to examples where people demonstrate respect for others. It's not enough to talk about respect. We all regularly need to remember what respect looks like in action if we're going to make it a part of our way of relating to others.

48.

Promote a Learning
Environment

There is nothing that fosters a learning environment more than focusing first and foremost on academic goals for each student. When little is expected from students, they have no reason to perform. Conversely, when students find themselves learning from teachers who believe that the students can succeed, the students show a far greater interest and success in learning.

Some of this has to do with self-esteem. A student who is surrounded by leaders who believe in his or her ability to succeed will have a higher estimation of self than one who is not. In fact, research has shown that students who are made to understand that they are capable of less than their peers actually perform at lower levels, even when their natural abilities are equal to others'.

The issue involves more than self-esteem, though. When a teacher and institution put learning first, this attitude is reflected in the way that a school and its individual classrooms are run. Academic success is openly rewarded. Distractions and disruptions in class time are kept to a minimum. The academic growth and development of students receives more attention and resources than the successful sports team or the high-profile events associated with the institution.

Your own interest and focus on learning will do more than anything else to motivate your students. If, when they ask a question, you respond in a way that encourages them to discover and learn for themselves, rather than handing over the answer, they'll see that you care about the learning process as much as the outcome in grades or scores. When you delight in the academic progress of successful students and go to great lengths to help students who are not progressing, you show that learning is both esteemed and expected.

49.

Practice Patience

Teaching calls for patience. At times, you need to apply it to your students. They don't catch on. They won't listen. They resist your every effort to teach and relate to them. You try, try, and try again. With many students, the effort pays off. With a few, it never does, or at least never appears to. In either case, your patient perseverance is the difference between success and failure.

At times, you need to apply patience to your administrators. They don't adequately understand the needs of the classroom. Their agendas seem opposed to what you are doing. They don't catch on. They won't listen. If you lose your cool or your determination to keep communicating, you have little or no hope of seeing positive change. If you exercise the patience to remain professional in a personally challenging situation, you'll not only increase your odds of success, but you'll feel better about yourself.

Sometimes, fellow teachers try your patience. They compete for limited resources. They jockey for status or recognition. They hide their own incompetence behind complaints about you. You may be able to build bridges with compassion, cooperation, and compromise. Without patience, you only feed the tensions.

You also need to be patient with yourself. You have your own learning challenges: the special needs of a new student, the technical aspects of a multimedia presentation or an electronic grading system, new curricula, or your own health and chemistry. If you lose patience with yourself, you add guilt, anger, and self-loathing to whatever other challenges you're facing. Far better to acknowledge human frailty, give yourself a break, and return to the fray. Only then can you learn from your mistakes, pick up the pieces, and make positive strides forward.

Where does this well of patience come from? It comes from the same source that helps you meet all of the challenges of teaching— your love of your students and your subject. If you're not in the business of teaching for the good of your students, stop now. If you are, remind yourself of that every time you're tempted to give up. It's what makes all of your experiences and frustrations worthwhile.

50.

Seek External Support

The teaching profession is an odd mix of group effort and solitary instruction. We have a support group of colleagues, but we almost always prepare and present solo. We aren't viewed by our students as one of a corps of teachers, but as the one who holds all of the cards for what they learn, how well it's taught, and how they are evaluated.

A potential side effect of the teaching profession is the temptation to take the solo route too far and play the "expert." We get used to the deference paid us by students and their parents, the friends and family who regard our profession highly, various people who have to answer to us—all of these people feed our hidden ego. We may come to believe the myth of intelligence or expertise that others spin.

The downside of this is the temptation to play the expert beyond your realm of expertise. No advanced degree in education or a particular academic discipline qualifies you to handle all of the issues and problems that accompany teaching. Yet when you face a problem or are sought out as a source of wisdom, you may succumb to handling it alone.

One of the surest signs of your wisdom as a teacher is your willingness and ability to recognize when you need help to do your job. Whether you're dealing with difficult behavior, an unidentified learning disability, a student's psychological problems, or disruptive cultural tensions, the time can come that you find yourself in over your head. If you are wise, you'll immediately seek support from people qualified to address the issue that you face.

Don't let pride get in your way. Before things get out of hand, seek out specific individuals or agencies that could be of help to you. Confide in those who can share responsibility for resolving the issues. Prove to your students and colleagues that you are indeed the professional that they believe you to be.

51.

Update Your Subject Matter

For both your own sake and the sake of your students, keeping the material that you teach fresh and up-to-date is vital. While the core content of a given discipline may not change, the times in which you teach continually change. The students that you have today live in a different world from the students that you taught five or ten years ago. How they relate to a subject is in constant flux. The vocabulary of their experience is unique to the place, culture, and times in which they are living and learning. To teach your subject in just one way is to ignore a changing world and an evolving student population.

For the teacher, a far more personal and compelling need is at work. When you pull out the same old lesson plans for recycling, you shortchange yourself. At some point in your preparation and teaching, you approached what you taught with the energy of an explorer. You still had to master the subject, and you had to discover a style and approach for your teaching that would suit both you and your students. The need to figure it all out added a constructive element to your work that communicated excitement and adventure to your students. It is the loss of such challenge that contributes to teacher burnout and classroom doldrums.

Students will easily pick up on your lack of excitement and will absorb it rather quickly. Students are always testing and measuring the relevance of what they are being taught. If they can find no connection to themselves or the world in which they live, they will tune you out. On the other hand, find ways to make the here-and-now an intrinsic part of your material, and you'll hold those students in the palm of your hand.

Real education is a living experience. Whether you involve yourself in subject-specific seminars, continue to take graduate courses, or make yourself an ongoing scholar with personal research and exploration, you can keep adding to your knowledge and understanding. When you add to that a lively interest in what's happening in your community, your country, and the world, the relevance of your material will become increasingly clear.

52.

Be Open to New Ideas

I t's easy to become jaded when your past attempts to do something different have failed. You let good opportunities pass you by because you've decided already that they can't pay off. You don't have to succumb to cynicism, but it takes an effort to remain open.

You need to face your disappointments and understand the temptation to give up that follows in their wake. This sometimes means jumping right into another new idea, before the fear of failure has a chance to settle in. It also means mustering the courage to learn from your mistakes. When you evaluate what goes wrong, you build the tools and understanding to take on ideas that stand a better chance of working out.

Of course, some of us naturally gravitate toward the tried and true. In that case, consider baby steps in some new directions. Promise yourself to listen to or search out at least one new idea pertaining to your teaching in the coming week. Then put yourself to the task of giving the idea serious consideration. A closed mind can become a powerful habit—but habits, by their very nature, can be broken.

53.

Make Everyone a Winner

Those in the business of encouraging positive relationships—psychologists, management consultants, diplomats, and mediators —will all tell you the same thing: People are at their best when their self-esteem is high and their sense of security is strong. When, on the other hand, they feel uncertain of themselves—when they question their intrinsic value and relative abilities—they are at their least effective and worst behaved.

Unfortunately, one of the downsides of a capitalist society is the extent to which competition and comparison permeate the overall tenor of our relationships. We grow up hearing, in one way or another, that our future success depends, at least in part, on how much better we are than the next person. The emphasis in our educational system on test scores and performance contests of one kind or another reinforce an underlying message that some students are better than others—that is, "winners." The only way that "losers" can become winners in such a system is for them to surpass others.

As a teacher, you want to encourage students to have a realistic view of their strengths, weaknesses, achievements, challenges, skills, and knowledge. You want to challenge them to stretch for growth and improvement. To some extent, you're stuck with the system that constantly compares one student or school with another. In your classroom, however, you can engender an atmosphere that builds on a healthier, more effective way of achievement. You can create a classroom dynamic that emphasizes the value of each individual and encourages cooperation, trust, and mutual benefit.

Look for ways to make sure that the success of one student doesn't demand the failure of another. Build opportunities for students to applaud one another's improvement instead of emphasizing grades and scores. Develop group projects and challenges that depend on mutual aid and shared successes. Never compare one student—in terms either of achievement or behavior—to another. Most of all, use every means at your disposal to uphold each student's self-esteem and sense of security in your classroom.

54.

Seek to Understand
the Administrator

Your feelings toward the administrators of your institution are bound to be complicated. Their function may cause you feelings of anxiety, resistance, caginess, or anger. You may also carry emotions into your relationship with your administrators that have to do with authority in general. In some cases, these include respect and appreciation. Just as likely, they include distrust and fear.

Like it or not, your administrators are here to stay. You and your fellow teachers don't have the time or energy to run a school at large while still fulfilling your specific teaching responsibilities. The administrators serve a crucial function.

Keeping that in mind, it's important that you seek to understand the concerns and demands that administrators face. They have reasons—good reasons, from their perspective—for their choices and demands. The more you know and understand the reasons, the more likely it is that you'll be able to appreciate what the administrators are trying to do. With that knowledge, you may also find that your choices have a significant impact on your administrator's ability to fulfill obligations to the institution at large. Realizing your impact may help you to respond constructively to things that you would otherwise find irritating.

Think in terms of communicating your concerns and desires as effectively as possible. If you have problems with the way that your supervisors treat you or support your efforts, you can't assume that they are cavalierly ignoring your reactions. They may not know your reactions. They'll only find out if you tell them. Granted, an administrator might listen with only half an ear to the complaints or needs of a single faculty member, but if you have significant concerns, there's a very good chance that others do, too. Regular discussions with colleagues and a united voice can open ears and doors that would otherwise remain closed.

The more you can develop lines of communication between faculty and administrators, and the more you can keep an open mind to the administrators' underlying concerns, the better your attitude is likely to be. With a better attitude, the relationship between faculty and administrators can become one of the strongest agents of constructive change and mutual service.

55.

Be Sensitive to
External Trouble

You know who your challenging students are, and you know which students typically make your job easy. When cooperative students turn silent, sullen, rebellious, or troublesome, you can be left scratching your head.

Such moments are likely to arise with any student, eventually. They may come and go in the same way that moods crop up and then pass. They may represent a predictable phase in a student's development, depending upon their age and circumstances. Or they may grow out of frustrations in your class, either with the material that you're presenting or another class member. Always remember that negative changes can also signal troubles outside of the classroom.

Such a situation calls for your patience and forbearance. When you encounter negative changes in a student, take a breath before you lose your confidence or your cool. Take the time to see if the negative phase passes, watching to look for explanations for the changes that you see. If the negative change persists, you may find that a direct approach is the most helpful. There's nothing wrong with taking a few minutes with a student to express concern. Saying, "You haven't been yourself lately. Is there some way I can help?" signals that you care enough to notice the change, even if the student chooses not to explain. Of course, you may get the straight story. In that case, you have the information that you need to make a difference on behalf of that student, if only by being a good listener. If not, having broached the subject will at least give you something to build on if trouble persists.

Be sensitive to troubles that a student may be dealing with outside of your class. If possible, check with others who know the individual and his or her circumstances. Consider that your classroom may be a haven from problems in the person's private life. The last thing that you want to do is make things worse. Invest the effort needed to understand what's going on and be a force for positive change in the student's life.

56.

Create an Environment of Safety

Teaching is about a lot of things—a body of knowledge that you want your students to grasp; a set of values that you hope to convey; specific skills that they need to master; and probably, a certain quality of relationships that you want to foster.

All of these goals have their place in education, and it's up to you as a teacher to find the best ways to achieve them. However, if your students do not feel safe when they enter your classroom, no amount of effort or skill on your part will make up the difference. People instinctively seek to satisfy their most basic needs first.

Safety in the classroom takes many forms, and you need to communicate to your students that in all ways, it is a priority for you. They need to know that you will not tolerate any physical or verbal mistreatment, that you are personally trustworthy, and that you can be counted on to address their fears and anxieties. They also need to understand that you have the power to protect them.

Safety is not only a matter of physical or emotional freedom from attack or harm. Your students need consistency and predictability in both your attitudes and behavior in matters related to security. The structure and order that you maintain communicates to them that you are in control—a vital element in their sense of security. The limits that you set assure them that they are in good hands, even when they are tempted to push those limits. The strength of purpose and character that you exhibit comforts them even when they put it to the test.

Safety also includes guarding your students' dignity and self-esteem. Students are highly unlikely to take academic risks unless they know that they have your support, no matter how successful the outcome. You create a safe environment for growth and development when you make it clear that you respect every effort and will not accept teasing or demeaning responses from others in the group.

The need to feel safe runs deep in the human psyche. Meet this need in your classroom, and you will open the way to an environment that encourages students to want to achieve.

57.

Be the Adult

M ost of us harbor a child within us who appears when we are emotionally volatile. Such moments may arise out of childhood memories. They may be due to old angers, insecurities, or frustrations. Whatever their specific source, they have the power to subvert our own best efforts to model the behavior and attitudes that we hope to encourage in our students.

No matter what the age of your students, you are certain to deal with childish behavior in them from time to time. Their immaturity can be exasperating enough that it will elicit an equally childish response from you. When you meet this kind of behavior with the same response, you get nowhere. Your discussion or exchange is reduced to a playground fight.

The best defense you have against falling into battle with your students is self-awareness. When you find yourself losing control, take note. Pinpoint the occasion and the moment that pushes you over the edge. Pay attention to what specifically is said, implied, or done that you find difficult to tolerate. When you've identified the source, go another step and ask yourself why that particular thing sends you hurtling back into your immature self. When you reach this level of consideration, you can begin to bring a mature attitude and behavior to your problem.

Keep in mind that when children act like children, they depend on you to be the adult. They look to you for ways to resolve what they lack the maturity to resolve. And they learn step by step how to move into new levels of maturity with you as their model. When older students act like children, they benefit in the moment and over time from your ability to rise above childishness.

Be the adult in your classroom. You will defuse some of the silliness that gets in the way of a constructive learning environment. You will model positive alternatives to behavior and attitudes that stand in the way of growth and development. And you will earn the respect and trust of the people that you teach.

58.

Promote Bonds

Friction or animosity between students in a class can create a powerful distraction to learning. It makes sense, then, that if you can find ways to build stronger, more constructive relationships in your classroom, you will not only improve the atmosphere within your group, but you will also improve the success rate of individual students.

Perhaps the most effective means of building bonds among your students is to incorporate opportunities for cooperative learning. The tried-and-true group project allows for a division of labor among students while providing a goal or reward that they pull toward together. Students have to rely on one another and often learn to encourage one another for the sake of mutual success. Similarly, small study and discussion groups tend to foster bonds that build each individual's self-esteem and skills.

Any way that you can encourage students to work together will promote a positive experience for them that enriches their education better than any curriculum. To make the most of cooperative learning and the bonds that it builds, keep a few caveats in mind. First, a learning group should be as representative of your class makeup as possible, mixing genders, ethnicities, and abilities. Such a mixing can break down prejudices and assumptions that traditional cliques build and perpetuate. It can also bring slower students along at a faster pace and encourage faster students to exercise leadership. Second, make sure that projects are designed in such a way that cooperation by all members of the group is necessary. The leader types are apt to take over—and the lazy or insecure types are likely to allow them to—unless you make it impossible. Third, provide a measure for both individual and group assessment. You don't want to frustrate a student by failing to recognize his or her level of involvement and effort, regardless of the group's success. Finally, leave some room in cooperative assignments for fun. One of the potential benefits of group work is the element of play in it that can build bonds and enhance the experience at the same time.

The idea of cooperative learning rests on a foundation that emphasizes positive relationships as much as it does academic achievement. As you build strong bonds among your students and find ways to let them learn and perform together, you are helping them learn essential life skills. They are gaining valuable experience in setting and reaching goals as a team.

59.

Tolerate No Cruelty

Cruelty rears its ugly head in many guises, but whether it appears in the form of teasing, goading, verbal abuse, or physical threats, you have a moral and professional duty to stop it. By your unequivocally negative response to any and all cruelty, you leave students in no doubt about what they can expect in your classroom. If there are students who have regularly been mistreated at school or at home, you will create a safe haven for them. You will show them that possibilities other than cruelty exist for them. If students have an essentially healthy attitude and behave relatively well toward others, you will reinforce their positive relationship skills and steer them away from the influence of bullies and teases. If you are working with students who treat others in cruel ways, you will provide the moral yardstick they need to understand that what they are doing is wrong and why.

Cruelty during childhood creates misery, self-doubt, and fear. It can cause depression, rage, suicide, and acts of violence toward others.

It has such a profound effect that if you are dealing with cruelty among your students, it's worth taking valuable class time to deal with it directly. If you have questions about how to approach the problem, call on professional counselors to help you.

Keep in mind that when you strive to eliminate a destructive behavior, you increase your rate of success if you teach better communication and relationship skills at the same time. This may mean working relentlessly with a student who shows tendencies toward cruelty. You may find that such a student has been abused in the past and has taken on the behavior as a defense. The student needs both consistent feedback and the influence of alternative behaviors.

Dealing with cruelty may also mean teaching a student how to avoid being the victim. Here again, if you have questions about how best to do this, let professionals help you. You may be the voice that breaks a cycle of pain and misery in another person's life. Cruelty is serious business. Treat it as such the moment that it appears.

60.

Make the Most of Multimedia

With the tremendous resources in technology available to the average classroom today, there is little excuse for not putting them to use. Because nearly all schools set a high priority on computer literacy, most students have the opportunity to use learning software and do Internet research. In addition, TVs and the video technology that comes with them have made substantial inroads into the classroom. By all means, take every advantage of these advances in technology. Use what is offered and go in search of new ways to make the most of it. Log some Internet time on your own to identify some of the programming and web sites that could enhance the classroom and homework experience for your students.

Don't stop with technology. Remember that some of the old-fashioned media have a lot to offer, as well. Watch out for live performances in the arts in your area and investigate what it would take to make one part of a class experience. With a little imagination, you can translate music, theater, dance, or the visual arts into enrichment for math, science, history, economics, or language classes just as surely as you can for arts-related courses. Look, as well, at what it would take to bring a performer into your classroom or school. Live performance is all the more important now when so many people have more virtual experiences than they do real time and space experiences.

Make sure you know what's available. Then find ways to use as much of it as you can. Consider the special museums, planetariums, botanical gardens, and zoos in your area. And don't forget such old-fashioned media as radio, newspapers, and magazines. In fact, when students become adept in the use of high-tech gadgets, you may find ways in which they can produce their own radio presentations, newsletters, magazines, or journals. People who don't find standard curricula compelling will sometimes light up when they are offered a media-centered alternative.

61.

Let Your Humanity Show

When your students gather in your class, they are at your mercy in many regards. They have to answer to you in regard to their academic performance, and their general behavior, attitudes, and sometimes even appearance. This can make a student feel exposed and vulnerable, especially when the chips are down, because it is not a reciprocal arrangement.

You can help empower your students emotionally by allowing your own humanity to show through your role of teacher. It's okay to let students know that you get tired or cranky sometimes. You can speak honestly about your personal experience as a student—your failures, as well as your successes—and thereby establish common ground for talking about the frustrations and challenges that your students may be experiencing. And you can be frank about your personal investment in the job you are doing.

Allow your vulnerability to peek through sometimes. You may discover that some of your students find it easier to trust you, as a result.

62.

Share Yourself

When you create assignments for your students that invite them to share who they are, make yourself a part of the assignment, as well. You may simply want to respond to their assignments with some small anecdote of your own. You may want to make a point of asking questions that allow you to respond in some personal way. Or you may want to do the assignment in abbreviated form. This has the benefit of letting your students get to know you while you model for their own contributions.

Sharing yourself can also be as simple as bringing your favorite goodie to class for a tasting. It can be displaying photographs of a trip you've taken, or playing a recording of music that you've seen performed live. The appearance of one of your family members, even briefly, can capture your students' curiosity and interest.

Each of your students has a relationship with you, and each decides how he or she is going to respond to you. Show them what you're about, and they'll have much more to build on.

63.

Write Notes

Many students have expressed their frustration and confusion over a class led by a teacher who does not communicate often or fully enough. They miss the fine points of an assignment, or they misunderstand how their work will be evaluated. They do their assigned work and hand it in, only to receive it back from the teacher with a poorly explained low grade.

It takes time to put instructions and meaningful responses in written form. It nonetheless is the most effective way to know that your message is received and understood. Some students are better visually than aurally. For them, seeing what you want to communicate is essential. They simply will not effectively take in what you say. When you put your communication in writing, you also create a record that you can refer to with your student, should the need arise.

Some teachers have found it useful to establish an in-class memo system whereby they communicate at least once a week by notes (either on paper or via e-mail, depending on your facilities). They may have a beginning- or end-of-week communication designed to inform or remind students of what's coming up. These communications may help students who have a hard time staying on task. For such students, if they are still minors, notes to parents or legal guardians may be a good idea, as well.

Pay special attention to how you mark any work turned in by your students. Remember that their finished work represents some effort on their part. Your response, or lack of it, can profoundly affect their motivation for future assignments. They need to know that you did your share of work when you graded their assignments, and they need to understand what you are saying about the quality of what they've done, in praise or critique, so that they can learn.

Don't forget that notes can be used to cheer and encourage, too. If you know of a birthday, make it a point to send a birthday greeting. If a student does an especially good job, rises to a particularly tough challenge, or has a success outside of your classroom, offer him or her praise in writing. There's something uniquely convincing about what a teacher is willing to commit to writing, and a student always appreciates being acknowledged as a success.

64.

Invite Student Offerings

You may provide regular opportunities for students to make formal presentations or be involved in assigned discussions and debates. Do you include the things that are important to them that may not, strictly speaking, be relevant to what you teach them? These ancillary interests can offer important, useful insights into the lives of your students.

Most people enjoy sharing what they care about or do well, but many people, young and old, have few natural opportunities to do so. Let your classroom be such a place. This does not need to use up an inordinate amount of class time. Perhaps one class period a month, you might allow time for student-sponsored enrichment. Figure out how many students need to have a chance in a single session so that every student can potentially be heard from before your teaching time with them is over.

You're likely to have at least a handful of students who are ready and willing to get involved. Let them lead the way so that more reticent students are encouraged to do likewise. You may want to make such an offering completely voluntary. In that case, you might have some class members that never participate as presenters. Or you may want to make it all-inclusive. In that case, make sure that you design the opportunity in such a way that everyone can feel comfortable. One of the top five fears among people in general is the fear of public speaking. You don't want such an exercise to be someone's worst nightmare come true. You simply want to bring the whole person into sight.

You may also find that giving a student or group of students an opportunity to be "teacher" once in a while is an excellent way to let them express themselves. Class work can be fun and creative when students get to teach. And students may gain more respect for the challenges that you face every day as their teacher.

Each of your students has something to offer, given a chance. You build students' self-esteem when you open your classroom to them for sharing what interests them.

65.

Make Learning a Group Event

The group project and small study group approaches can add a lot to your teaching environment. They challenge students to participate in the lesson in a more active way. Students learn academic discipline and an attitude of cooperation. But at times it's important to encourage the entire group to interact together, when you're presenting new material or really exploring new ideas.

Consider the model of a creative team in business or the arts. A team of people come together with a specific goal or outcome in mind. They take time in conversation to consider how to define the problem. They brainstorm to find a variety of ways in which they might solve the problem they have defined. Then they refine their ideas together, choosing the one or two strongest solutions and discussing how to implement them.

Such a model provides a promising scheme for adding variety and challenge to your class time, regardless of the subject matter. Many subjects lend themselves to the problem-solving method; it is not limited to math or science labs. When you engage your students in this way, you draw them into a creative process that develops skills that they will never learn from a lecture. Without knowing it, they learn to think logically for themselves and make connections. They discover how to draw conclusions about what they don't know from what they do know. They may even begin to appreciate the value of having more than one "head" to work on a problem—the bonus of cooperative effort.

In essence, when you engage students in creative group problem-solving, you teach them how to learn. In some cases, you have the privilege of watching them "get it" right before your eyes. Keep the dynamic of group learning in mind. It can encourage your students to do more work using their own initiative.

66.

Develop Conversation
Opportunities

Discussion and conversation are not the same thing. Formal discussions have a specific purpose and aim at a particular outcome. They tend to be structured and carry the weight of academic performance. Conversation is less formal and allows—by its nature—opinions, feelings, non sequiturs, and ideas. Discussion has a serious undertone. Conversation tends to be more relaxed. Making time to converse with your students can be a great aid to understanding, sympathy, and rapport in the classroom. Yet many teachers steer away from unstructured talk for fear that they will lose control of the group. While this is a possible outcome, it is not inevitable. You have it in your power to prevent this. A carefully orchestrated time of "free" conversation can give you tremendous opportunities to coax otherwise uninvolved students into participating.

The truth is that some students resist formal participation. It may be that they feel uncertain of their contribution and fear ridicule. Or they may be shy and find speaking to a group terrifying. They may even have a chip on their shoulder or a desire to rebel against "work." In any of these cases, you may find that your best efforts to pull them into a classroom discussion will fall flat.

But what happens when the stakes seem lower? Sometimes the most reticent students begin to open up. They may start timidly, but the more opportunities they have to make a small contribution to the group's chatter, the more confidence they build. Over time, you can actually recreate the rapport and relaxed atmosphere of informal conversations with a more serious subject at the core. Quiet students, who will have experienced some success at being open with the group, enter into the talk without realizing that they've crossed a new threshold.

Be brave. Let them talk sometimes. Think of yourself as a shepherd, turning your flock of students loose in a meadow of ideas and possibilities. They can graze at will, while you gently keep them within the borders with leading questions or comments of your own. You may be surprised at how the group warms up over time.

67.

Encourage Opinions

Anybody can parrot facts and figures, but it takes thought to absorb "canned knowledge" and form an opinion about it. Much of the standardized testing for which today's students are so arduously prepared tests their ability to take in, comprehend, and feed back information. Relatively few opportunities are structured into most classrooms for students to form and offer opinions on the material that they have learned.

Questions of opinion can vary widely. They can focus on history. ("What would you have done if you had been the president in that situation?") They can explore principles of education. ("Why do you think we study calculus?") They can encourage creative responses to literature. ("What would have happened if Peter Rabbit had not gotten away from Mr. McGregor?") Or they can focus on citizenship of one sort or another. ("What kind of dress code would you write for this school?") There's no limit to the subjects that lend themselves to this sort of student involvement.

Eliciting opinions from your students has the great advantage of forcing them to involve themselves personally in the subject at hand. Because you aren't asking for a preformed answer, they have to think through what they say. Of course, they may arrive with a preconceived opinion on some subject. In that case, you'll get to know them and their world a little better. You'll also have the chance to challenge their assumptions and suggest some alternative points of view for them to consider.

Opinions don't have to be "correct" to be valuable and instructive. In truth, opinions are not facts; people in a free society are entitled to their own opinions. It's important that you stress this without neglecting the fact that some opinions show more thought or moral judgment than others, and some are based on better data. Teach your students to back up their opinions with facts and sound reasoning, and you will have accomplished a great task indeed.

The more opinions you can elicit from your students, the better job you're doing in the classroom. Having an opinion means that a student has pinned him- or herself down. Expressing that opinion means that a student has mustered the courage and confidence to take a stand on something. Once the student does that, there's no stopping his or her growth.

68.

Recognize Effort

We live in a time and educational culture that places enormous emphasis on outcomes. We stress final scores, class ranks, cumulative grade-point averages, awards, trophies, and pennants. We show relatively less interest in perseverance, elbow grease, and reliability. That's a shame, because most of us actually value the latter qualities. Yet unless they result in a star performance, we often forget to give them their due.

The truth is that you probably won't often have more than a handful of stars in a class. That's why average is called "average." Most students fall in the midrange. Some of them are middling students for lack of effort. Others show average results after investing a lot of hard work. In fact, the mediocre student may put in far more work than the very bright student who comes easily to academic success.

The same mix of bright and average, hardworking and lazy, exists in many arenas. It doesn't stop in school. Some of your students will become college presidents, CEOs, high-ranking political leaders, and highly skilled professionals. Many others will fill the "ordinary" jobs that surround us every day—mail deliverers, store clerks, gas station workers, and janitors. Some of the stars will be stars indeed, people whom one can respect and trust. Some will be lazy, mean, or crooked. Some will do their job with such verve and integrity that it's a joy to deal with them; others will be surly, sloppy, or on the take.

You are part of the process that readies new generations of citizens for the responsibilities and challenges of adulthood. Some of what they learn to value comes from you and your classroom. What are you teaching your students about the relative value of natural smarts and stardom versus honest hard work? Don't just hand out kudos for the high performers. Make a point of recognizing and honoring the genuine efforts of even the most humble students.

69.

Promote the Underdog

Every group has its unofficial ranking—the stars, the jokers, the slow and steady, and the underdogs. Once students have been labeled by peers or administrators, it can be very hard for them to break free of that assigned place in the hierarchy. Unfortunately, teachers sometimes support the status quo, leaving the underdogs discouraged and defeated.

You don't need to cave in to the social pressure to keep an underdog under. In your class, you can give the underdog a promotion. When you break with consensus, you change the overall dynamic. Someone has something different to say about this student.

When you are delegating tasks in your classroom, look for jobs that your underdog can succeed at. Communicate that what you are asking for is important to you, and make a point of praising the work when the student has completed it. If there are situations in which the student does not excel, let your underdog take one of the assisting roles. Acting as one of your assistants can raise self-esteem and confidence.

Think of how you conduct interactive class time. Do you design your class participation in such a way that you inadvertently favor the gifted or popular students and discourage the underdogs? Consider ways that you can even the playing field in class, at least some of the time, so that students who feel left out have a chance to participate and make a meaningful contribution.

Discuss an underdog with other teachers or advisors who come into contact with him or her. It's easy to share complaints about students, but it doesn't help them grow. If, instead, you initiate the conversation in terms of how to help the underdog, you can turn the tide of attention that student receives from faculty and administrators.

A lot of underdogs leave school to become confident and successful professionals. That doesn't make the pain of their school experience any less at the time, however. Many, many people have looked back to school days and been grateful that they are over. And then there are those who look back with gratitude for that one teacher who saw something different in them and made them believe in themselves in a new way.

70.

Defuse Tension

Students of any age can rub one another the wrong way. They may heat up over personality conflicts, misbehavior, or opposing points of view on a heavy subject. Whatever the cause, their disputes can cause tension and distract the group from what you're teaching.

You may feel your own stress increase when your students act up. If so, don't beat yourself up over it. You're only human. If tension in the classroom tends to lead to an angry response, you need to take a step back now, when you're not in the midst of it, and think about constructive alternatives. To respond in anger will only intensify the troublesome situation.

Start by remembering that it is your job to lead, not to be led. Part of your leadership responsibility centers on what kind of atmosphere will prevail in your classroom. If you intend to maintain an atmosphere of order, calm, and courtesy, you have to model behavior that is appropriate to such an atmosphere. If you don't act out what you want, you've lost the battle at the outset.

Second, distinguish between the presenting problem and the actual source. You may observe a young student apparently throw the first kick, for example, when in fact the other student provoked the action at some unseen moment. The only way that you'll get to the bottom of it is to speak privately to the students involved. So as not to make matters worse or derail an entire class, your best course will probably be to separate the students physically, effectively creating a "timeout" without stopping the entire class.

With older students, the presenting problem may be rudeness or disrespect in a heated debate. A simple after-class question to each student (alone and out of earshot), such as, "So what was up, Charlie?" may give you some insight, regardless of how honest the answer is. In the moment, however, you're best served to move the discussion on, interrupting the debate in some good-natured way. "Excuse me," you may say. "This is fascinating, but we need to move on to another point right now. We'll get back to this in a bit." Fulfill the promise with a written exercise or some other nonconfrontational method.

Your most important role in a heated situation is to douse the flame. You can take the time when tempers cool to find ways to avoid further conflict between the participants. But unless you want your entire class time to be at the mercy of the combatants, your first duty is to lead the way back to courtesy.

71.

Count to Ten . . . Ten Times!

Anger—in particular, your anger—can be an issue in the classroom. In many cases, the circumstances in which you act out feelings of anger are not the actual source of the outburst. You may have been accumulating your anger over time, building up stress and irritation that in its small increments seemed manageable, but in the aggregate pushes you over the edge.

You can begin to change a pattern of temperamental outbursts when you learn to identify and deal with the seemingly small sources of anger as they occur. That means that you don't simply let them go. If there's something about a certain student that really pushes your buttons, figure out why. Does the student remind you of something in yourself that you don't like? Or does the student exemplify something that arouses your envy or makes you feel disrespected?

Perhaps you have allowed a schedule or situation that is particularly stressful for you to sap your inner resources. Even if you can't force immediate changes, you can make your needs known and insist that over time changes be made. You can work with your administration or fellow teachers to devise a strategy for making your situation less stressful. Just taking some kind of action can alleviate some of the stress because you no longer feel helpless.

Whatever the root causes of anger in your professional life, you can take steps to manage your behavior. First of all, whatever you do, don't be mad at yourself for feeling angry. Anger is part of our emotional makeup, so welcome to the human race. You only heap anger upon anger when you're disappointed that you aren't the exception. Second, deal with things as they occur. Resolve conflicts as they come up, or at least acknowledge them and decide how long you'll wait before resolution is needed. Respond to specific irritations by looking for ways to lessen or eliminate them before they have a chance to accumulate.

Before you act out your anger, count to ten once to let the adrenaline rush pass. Count to ten a second time to give careful thought to whatever has brought your anger to the surface. Count to ten a third time to respond in the moment with a clear head. Then give yourself some real time (another seven counts of ten, at least, when you're away from the situation) to think ahead to how you want to handle such provocation in the future.

72.

Practice an Open-Door Policy

Your students feel the same range of emotions as you do. On top of that, many of them understand that in some regards, they are at your mercy. Unless they know that they have your ear when they need it, such vulnerability can lead to a variety of stresses in your classroom.

Make it a policy to be available to your students for help and feedback. Set aside certain times when they can have a private word with you. This may mean allowing five-minute conferences before roll call, before or after lunch, during study halls, or at the end of the school day. Make sure that you provide times for students who can't stay after school because of sports or transportation troubles.

You can also arrange to have "office hours" by phone at prearranged after-school times. Perhaps one early evening a week, you can make appointments.

Your open door spells investment in your students. When they know that they can come to you, their frustrations may become more manageable.

73.

Spell Out Consequences

Most teaching situations require a certain set of rules and requirements to establish the goals of the class and quality of the class time. Standards for behavior and academic performance are laid out, and a student who fails to fulfill them pays a price of some kind. Depending on the age and maturity of your students, these standards and the consequences for not meeting them are actually part of the students' education. The students learn to equate action with consequence when they fail to study for an exam, let an assignment go until the last minute, speak out of turn, or skip too many classes. Their grades suffer, their work mounts up, or they receive embarrassing punishments.

You subvert both your standards and your students' potential learning curve when you fail to alert them to the consequences of noncompliance. Standards only hold up when you stick to them consistently and offer appropriate consequences when they are not met. That's rule number one. If your students don't understand what's at stake when they don't meet the standards, they have no way of gauging the importance or seriousness of your expectations.

When you set up the rules and requirements of your classroom, make sure that you have them clear in your own mind and that you establish the consequences—good and bad—ahead of time. Let your students in on this information right from the start, and assume that you'll need to spell it out more than once.

Ideally, you should put it in writing. Many high school and all college courses publish academic requirements in the class syllabus. School manuals spell out issues of participation and behavior. For younger students, make sure parents have all information in writing, as well. In addition, find various ways to repeat and reinforce what's expected and what happens when expectations are disappointed. You can save yourself a lot of confusion and frustration by giving your students every reason to stay with the program.

74.

Give Regular Feedback

Little frustrates and defeats a student more than to find out too late that he or she isn't on track in some way. That's why interim reports were developed in the first place. Reports that appear well before evaluations allow students the opportunity to get help, do makeup or extra-credit work, or simply work harder.

However, required interim reports rarely offer enough feedback for students to stay on top of what they need to improve. It's up to individual teachers to find as many ways as possible to keep their students in touch with their progress. The advent of technology and abundance of education-related software make this easier than ever to do, but even for the pen-and-pencil set, such feedback can spell the difference between a student's success and failure.

Make prompt response to homework and assignments a top priority. Handing graded work back in a timely manner allows your students to see specifically what you're looking for and whether they're delivering it. They have a chance to learn from their mistakes, as well as from your instruction. They also have the opportunity to improve sooner rather than later, because you haven't made them hand in several assignments before they get the first one back.

Create a student-by-student record of assignments, quizzes, tests, and projects. A spreadsheet of all that is required in a grading period helps students see their completed work mount up. Such a spreadsheet often marks a completed assignment by recording the grade. With many computer programs, it's even possible to show an up-to-date cumulative grade. Since most students seriously underestimate the effect of a zero (a missed assignment) or low individual grade on a cumulative grade, this can be remarkably effective.

Use some class time, when appropriate, to also offer feedback to the group as a whole on what people are doing that is working and what mistakes seem to be showing up a lot. This can uncover areas in which you may not be making the material or the assignments clear— you'll learn sooner rather than later how to help your students.

If you allow late work to be handed in, give students the heads-up on getting in their missing work while they still have time to recover. A last-minute alert can only add stress and discouragement to the mix for them. A timely reminder gives them a fighting chance.

Feedback is a gift to both the student and you. You can use it to improve both your teaching and their performance and save everyone needless grief.

75.
Offer Amnesty

Academic standards are important, and students need to know that they each bear individual responsibility for how they meet those standards. But sometimes, circumstances at home make it difficult or impossible for students to concentrate or keep up. Sometimes, a special event or family difficulty means critical time away from schoolwork over which the student has no power. Sometimes, students get sick. Sometimes, they fall behind at the outset and lack the skills to regroup, thus falling farther and farther behind.

There are times, too, when your expectations exceed your students' abilities to achieve. Either you have given too difficult an exam or assignment, or you did not make expectations clear enough for students to fulfill them. In either case, the fault is yours. You may not want to admit it, but they did their best with your flawed demands.

In one way or another, you have to face the fact that your students will sometimes not meet the minimum standards. Make sure that you are paying attention to the details associated with any student's failure to perform. You may be dealing with a student who rebelliously refuses to do the work. For such students, a hard line may be the only hope for rehabilitation. If they insist on learning the hard way, you do them a big favor when you let them do so.

Some students simply need more individual help, and it's part of your job to see that they get it. If they genuinely don't understand the material, the test questions, or the assignments, no amount of grading down will make a difference. They need more instruction, more time, and some individual attention. Sometimes, they need a break. There is little in a student's life that is more demoralizing than to realize that no matter how hard he or she works, the bad grades of their past are still there.

When you find students who are giving their best effort to improving past poor performance, but whose grade outcome is impossibly compromised, you can offer a big boost to morale and improvement by forgiving some of the past. You may choose to drop the lowest grade, allow a replacement assignment, or offer a one-time grade improvement. Without compromising standards, you'll be communicating that effort counts and the past does not dictate the present or the future. Sometimes, mercy is the better part of fairness. Encourage your struggling students with this gift.

76.

Give Credit for
Corrected Work

The story goes that Thomas Edison tried thousands of materials for a light bulb filament before he happened on a successful one. Legend has it that he proclaimed, "I haven't failed. I now know thousands of ways that don't work." He went on to advise, "Don't call it a failure. Call it an education."

What is your aim when you give your students exams and assignments? Is it to write another number into a grade book? Is it to show students what they still need to learn? Is it to certify a student as an "A," "C," or "F" level student? Or is it all of these and something more? Most teachers and administrators would choose the last answer. They would agree that graded work is meant not only to reveal a student's competence, but also to improve it. It stands to reason, then, that students benefit not only from the opportunity to review their work after the teacher has graded it, but also from the process of correcting what they've missed.

Some work can't formally be corrected or credited for corrections. For example, standardized tests function specifically as a benchmark assessment of what a student knows and how fast he or she works at the time of testing. Whatever the student achieves on the test in the first place stands for that testing occasion, without recourse. This is also true, generally speaking, of end-of-term testing.

Most of the work students hand in, however, does not fall into this category. With most assignments that students hand in, their mistakes have great educational potential—they serve to teach students what doesn't work, which in turn can lead them to what does work. But in order for education to grow out of mistakes, students need to be encouraged to review completed, graded work, and rethink what they've done incorrectly. What better incentive in a grading system can you offer students than grade credit for going through the process of identifying what they did wrong and correcting it?

Make the most of the assignments and tests that you give your students. If you let them correct assignments, you will not only milk extra mileage out of the material on their behalf, but you will also teach your students the value of perseverance.

77.

Know Your Goals

As a teacher, you juggle many demands and concerns from day to day. It's easy to lose sight of the big picture in the tangle of details that distract and wear you out. If you did not give serious thought to what the big picture was for you when you entered the teaching profession, you were lost from the outset. But even those who begin teaching with lofty goals—the vast majority—can lose their way.

One of the best ways to hold on to what you want to accomplish in the classroom is to clearly articulate your goals to yourself. It's possible to have a general idea of what you're aiming at without ever having formulated it in words. Language is a powerful tool, and putting your goals into a mission statement can give you new insight into what your work is really about for you.

So why are you teaching? What generally do you hope to accomplish in a teaching season for each of your students? For yourself? Make a point of writing down a single paragraph that answers these questions. Write it in such a way that someone who doesn't know you could read it and understand what you're saying. If you have any doubt about whether you've been clear or specific enough, test your statement by giving it to a colleague to read.

If your institution doesn't already require it, do the same thing for the specific goals that you have for individual units of study or particular assignments. You can easily fall into bad habits with content and approach to material that you've taught often without keeping a focus on what you hope to accomplish. By reiterating your goals, you bolster your strength of purpose and increase your reserves of patience and creativity.

Think about your goals for your individual students. How do you hope to see their lives change? Again, be specific. Look at your students one at a time and consider what each one needs in relation to what you teach and what you can hope to accomplish. When you know what you're doing and why, it becomes easier to make the daily choices and take the steps that will serve your students' best interests.

78.

Handle Problems
While They're Small

There are plenty of little things that cause stress in a teacher's life. Unfortunately, if you let the little things accumulate by ignoring or neglecting them, they can balloon into big problems that are not easy to resolve. The best way to keep this from happening is to face a potential problem right away, deal with it, and move on.

When you see the seeds of friction between two students, step in before it has a chance to escalate into real animosity. If you've established basic rules of courtesy and communication, you already have the basis for a constructive conversation. If you haven't set up such rules, do it now. Half the battle is teaching your students to communicate in a way that doesn't inflame sore feelings or encourage teasing.

When you note that a student has failed to turn in work, address it sooner rather than later. Missing work has a habit of snowballing on a student. If you wait to say something, you may find that your student has become paralyzed by a growing list of unfinished assignments. If you catch it early, you can help the student find time to get it done.

When you see a trend developing toward rowdiness during class time, blow the whistle right away. Don't go along with the fun in hopes of quieting things down later. It's important to have fun with your students and create an atmosphere that equates good times with learning, but both you and your class need to know that you are in control at all times. With a smile and a friendly tone of voice, bring the class to order and set up a system by which they are rewarded with planned fun only when they consistently respect the boundaries of classroom behavior.

The list of issues that you face daily as a teacher goes on and on. The examples above are meant only to illustrate the value and advantage of using your powers of observation to note and redirect the small problems while they're small. It's amazing how much stress you can save yourself with steady doses of preventive action.

79.
Find One-on-One Time

The notion of being accessible to each of your students can't be overemphasized. While an open door serves to let students initiate individual contact, it also falls to you to actively seek time with your students. It may seem daunting if you have a standard-sized group of public school students, especially if you teach multiple sections of a subject in middle or upper grades. Yet the business of education revolves around those students, and unless you know them well enough to have a sense of their needs, you can hardly expect to accomplish the primary mandate of your profession.

The conversations need not be long, and they can be spread out so that you meet with just one, two, three, or four students on any given day. You can plan such meetings during a free period, a study hall, or before or after class. With larger groups, you may have to be more creative, but don't let that stop you. If you need to use class time, seek administrative support in the form of classroom aides. Call on parents to be involved in overseeing in-class assignments that allow students to work independently or in small groups while you have short conversations with individuals.

If there are opportunities to be less formal about one-on-one time, by all means make the most of them. If you regularly call for a student helper, use such occasions to get to know your helper a little better. Take an interest in whatever he or she offers to tell you about. Let the conversation wander away from school-related business. There's no substitute for looking a student in the eye.

You gain surprising insights when you separate students from their cohorts. They relate to you without the pressure to perform that peers tend to engender, and you relate to them as other human beings, without the larger-than-life style you may use when presenting before the group. You humanize the classroom relationship and open the door to greater trust.

Your students are individuals. They know that. It's a gratifying notion to them when they find out that you know it, too, and respect them for it.

80.

Instill Goals in
Your Students

Many students show up in your classroom without any great purpose. School is mandatory—this is what they've been told they must do. Some students enjoy learning and going to school. Other students dislike the whole business and would happily be anywhere else in the world. Students' attitudes can be vastly improved if they begin to develop some specific goals for themselves during their time spent in school.

Imagine having someone say to you: "What you do today is going to radically change your life forever." Would you keep moving along without a thought? Probably not. The truth is that what your students do from day to day in school really will change the rest of their lives, for better or worse. You know that. Many of their parents and guardians know it. But most students don't. Even continuing education students may doubt the remarkable ways in which education can transform their future.

Awaken your pupils to the ways that their education will feed into all that follows. Encourage them to think about what lies ahead. Help them set goals. Give them a sense of what others have gained or lost through education. Find stories about people that they admire. Share your own experiences and those of students that you've observed in the past. Help them to think in terms of what they hope to get out of what you are all doing together.

The better you know your students, the better able you will be to guide them—but there are ways for you to help them even without intimate knowledge of their hopes and dreams. The most important thing you can communicate is simple: If they aim for nothing, they're very likely to hit their target.

81.

Use Your Breaks

When stress and anxiety build and your workload overtakes you, you are not at your best. The harder you push when your inner resources are low—when you're running on empty—the less efficient you become. The simplest tasks become chores that take unwieldy amounts of time. The big jobs look Herculean, tempting you to procrastinate and thus raise the stress level even higher. Creativity flies out the window. You'll use up energy and coping skills if you don't remedy the problem. It may be time to take a break.

Breaks serve several vital functions, most important of which is a renewal of perspective. You can't see the bigger picture when you're mired in stress. You have to stand outside of it, if only briefly, in order to recapture your sense of purpose and resolve. When you leave the scene, you see beyond the details that can make it hard or impossible to put first things first. You give yourself a chance to take stock and assess not only where you are and what you need to do, but what you hope for in the future. It's this last bit that can help you sort out how to tackle your immediate challenges. What you're aiming for will dictate how you arrange your priorities.

Almost as important, of course, is your physical well-being. Physical wellness is closely tied to emotional and psychological wellness, of course, but it also depends on adequate rest, nourishment, and exercise. These fuel all of your efforts to perform, yet they are often the first to be neglected when professional pressure is on. Breaks can and should give you the opportunity to get sleep, pay attention to what and when you eat, and assess whether your exercise routine is working for you. Breaks afford a good time to reinstate healthy habits of the past or invent new ones.

You may have other ideas in mind when you take time off from teaching, but if you don't give first place to reviving body and spirit, you will run out of fuel without fail. This is called "burnout," and the teaching profession is rife with it. So take your breaks, even when you don't think that you have time to do so. Refreshed and renewed by time away from the daily grind, you'll more than make up the difference when you return to work.

82.

Acknowledge Your Own Needs

One of the benefits of the perspective you gain when you take time off is the opportunity to reconnect with who you are and what you care most about. As you return to your old self, you get in touch with what is missing in your teaching life. Knowing what is amiss is the first, indispensable step to doing something about it.

Pay attention when you're hurting. Many of us try to deaden our receptors to our own pain rather than deal with it. We eat or drink too much, spend our free time mindlessly planted in front of a television, or fill our extracurricular time with enough noise and activity to drown out the signals of internal trouble. Don't do it. Pain, whether physical or psychological, plays a crucial role in human health and peak performance. You need to feel the pain, locate its source, and take meaningful action to deal with it.

Give yourself some quiet time. Listening is a learned skill, and listening to yourself requires solitude and the willingness to face what hurts, as well as what works. You may find it helpful to list all of the issues and relationships that come to mind when you look for sources of pain. From there, you can begin to assess why these cause pain and what changes will have to be put into action for you to improve the situation.

The next stage, of course, is to seek the needed changes. Perhaps this will be something that requires only your action. More often, however, changes require action and assistance from others. Acknowledging your needs to yourself must translate into acknowledging your needs to relevant others. Do you lack the resources to do your job properly? Tell your administrators so, and keep telling them. Have you been trying to handle something that requires expert assistance? Get help from a specialist. Are you stuck in a negative dynamic with people at work? Address it directly. Look for mediation. Change what you do, regardless of whether others are willing to change.

There's a good reason why the old saying, "The squeaky wheel gets the grease," has stuck around for so long. It's true. When you're needy, squeak. Acknowledge that you have needs to yourself and to others who can help meet them.

83.

Remember Your Students'
Competing Demands

In most educational institutions, guidelines exist regarding how much students should be expected to do outside of class. Such guidelines have been set up for good reason. On the one hand, they reinforce what students are learning in class. On the other, they are meant to pull in the reins on the overzealous teacher who would like to load up on the homework.

When you ask your students to use after-school time for your class, make sure that you remain within the limits allowed by your institution and common sense. Just as overload makes you stressed and inefficient, it subverts your students' abilities to learn and perform, as well. When you assign them more than is fair, you're effectively undoing some of the hard work that you've accomplished as their teacher.

Remember, too, that guidelines are just that. Simply because you can give a certain amount of homework doesn't mean you always should. For example, if you know that a big school event is coming up for your students—one that will involve a lot of their extra time for a short period—you may want to look for ways to give them a homework break. Allow some extra time in class to complete assignments. Select assignments that are less time-consuming. Or simply forgo homework for the time involved. This can apply to holidays, class trips, or performance dates for drama, music, or other events.

Your students have a variety of needs and demands from sources other than their teacher. Make yourself aware of the competition for your students' time. Think in terms of their welfare, as well as your lesson plans, and you'll have a healthier, happier group of people to teach.

84.

Question Labels

If the era of the 1960s and 1970s offered our culture anything, it taught us to think for ourselves. Slogans such as "question authority" and "question assumptions" reminded us that thoughtlessly accepting the values and beliefs of others—even our own families, church, or government—can be not only ignorant, but downright dangerous.

Questions have their place in educational institutions, as well. Over the course of a teaching career, you will be handed countless prepackaged ideas and assessments that concern your students. The students will often arrive in your class prejudged by exams, standardized tests, and previous teachers. You will be told what to expect from them academically, what learning differences they are believed to have, and what kind of behavior they exhibit. All of this is handed on to you, presumably to make your job easier and the classroom more efficient.

Beware. While such assessments can be invaluable and promote the success of individual students, they are fallible. All kinds of variables exist that can skew the accuracy of standard measures and labels. A student may be deemed "slow," but in fact is a very bright but very anxious test-taker. Another student may come to you with a reputation for bad behavior, the source of which was never identified. This student may need more than anything to be given a fresh start with a new teacher. A student with an apparent learning disability may actually have outgrown its effect and now be suffering from boredom because of inappropriately low placement.

By all means, make the most of assessments that others pass along to you, when you can, but never neglect to test the preconceptions. Students can get labeled and locked into their past reputations by others so that they finally give up trying to be any different. One of your important roles as teacher is that of assessor. You can see for yourself what a student is made of if you give him or her a chance to show you. Test the limits that others have applied to your students. Give them the benefit of a doubt. You may change the direction of a person's life in the process.

85.

Acknowledge Your Own Moods

While some folks are blessed with a relatively steady temperament, others suffer all of the ups and downs of volatility, and still others fall somewhere in the spectrum between these extremes. But no matter where you fall, you are likely to experience many moods in your lifetime. How you feel changes from day to day—at times, even moment to moment—depending on your physical well-being, stress level, circumstances, chemistry, and daily experiences. You will do well to keep this in mind as you prepare for class.

Before you begin class, take a moment to reflect. Take your temperature, so to speak. Are you tired? Hopped up? Angry? Do you feel edgy? Indifferent? Depressed? Many of us have developed the habit of putting our inner state out of our conscious thoughts. In the teaching profession, this can be self-defeating. We almost always create our lesson plans without reference to our state of being, because the planning doesn't take place at the time of the presentation. But it isn't helpful to neglect noting "where you are" when it comes time to teach. In fact, where you are when you enact your plans will have a profound effect on your style and ability to fulfill them.

Be aware of your frame of mind and spirit when you enter your classroom. Take it into account. Make adjustments for the sake of being effective. If need be, alter the way that you planned to teach. You may not have the psychological energy to fulfill an elaborate or unusual plan. Or you may have the flair to take a prosaic plan and spontaneously soup it up. In either case, your teaching will be improved by adjusting your style in keeping with your frame of mind.

86.

Seize Opportunities

Don't let the negative connotations of the term "opportunist" stop you from thinking like a positive opportunist. Surprises in the classroom can throw you for a loop, or they can be some of your best resources for a vital, engaging lesson.

Be prepared for those surprises that inevitably arise when you're dealing with people. Conflicts that flare up among students can be excellent opportunities for promoting skills for conflict resolution. Detours in a discussion can provide unexpected depth and relevance. An unexpected visitor can add variety to the day and potentially be a productive addition to your plans. In some cases, your best response to an unexpected opportunity for change is to lay aside your plans in lieu of something spontaneous.

Of course, not all opportunities come in the form of surprises. Make it a habit to look ahead as you plan your lessons. Have the calendar of your institution on one side and a standard calendar on the other. Take note of any unusual events, birthdays, or holidays coming up, and consider how they might relate to what you'll be teaching and the people in your class. Whether there's a guest speaker in another class, a special day for someone, or traditional festivities that you know some students will celebrate, you can incorporate them in your class time. Such additions to a traditional presentation of your material, however small, can be attention-getters that involve your students beyond their usual participation.

It has been said that when optimists are handed a lemon, they make lemonade. Be an optimistic opportunist on behalf of your students. You'll worry less, have a more interesting teaching experience, and convey some valuable lessons to your students about flexibility, positive thinking, and creativity.

87.

Create Benchmarks

Like you, your students need motivation for learning and performing that is relevant to them just as you need motivation for staying professionally sharp. You may be compelled by your own love of learning, your desire to make a positive difference in the lives of others, or your need to make a living. But what about your students? What keeps them at the job of studying, completing assignments, and involving themselves in the classroom dynamic?

Any way that you can fuel your students' motivation will repay itself many times over in improved performance and classroom interaction. One motivator that seems to help many people stay on task is establishing a way of tracking progress toward a well-defined set of goals. Athletes and people in fitness training do this with charts and graphs that track when, how, and to what extent they are training. People trying to lose weight may keep a record of both the food that they're consuming and the changes in their weight and measurements. People saving money for a big purchase or a community raising money for a project may devise a visual representation that allows them to see the money mounting up. All of these devices serve to remind the individuals of what they want to accomplish eventually and let them see how they're doing at the moment.

Consider what goals you want to emphasize with your students. Then create visual images of the progress that they are making. You can use a chart of their grades, a graph of work completed, or a folder in which completed work can impressively accumulate.

A benchmark can be applied to the group's progress as well. Devise a visual representation of what will be involved in a unit of study. It may be a map, a list, a graph, or a visual metaphor (a tree, a racetrack, a computer maze, or whatever). As you advance in the material you're studying together, mark off the "territory" covered. Students will find it rewarding and stimulating to see their progress.

The beauty of benchmarks is positive feedback. Unlike the typical interim report, which makes a point of what's missing, the benchmark emphasizes what's completed.

88.

Turn Failure into Learning

A fear of failure prevents many people from ever reaching beyond their safe zone. Despite great promise, they would rather maintain the status quo than try and fail. Most educational institutions, unfortunately, reinforce this fear to such an extent that some students actually develop physical ailments related to the stress produced. These institutions promote a perfectionist atmosphere that allows few students to shine. The process of learning becomes secondary to the grades and scores achieved, and the students who do not learn as quickly or easily as the top-scoring students stop reaching.

You can make your classroom a haven from the stress brought on by trying to be perfect. Your students look to you for a sense of what's expected from them. You may have standard expectations that need to be met, but you can communicate very clearly to your students that your primary goal is to see them meet their own potential.

One effective way of breaking down the fear of failure is to regularly challenge students with ungraded assignments. Give them work that they have to stretch for and reward them richly for trying, despite outcomes. Participating in a lesson that doesn't punish them for not getting it right will be a novel and freeing experience for many.

Consider ways in which you can take the failures of your students and turn them into learning opportunities. Investing the time and effort to explore how and why someone failed to "get it right" is often a major step toward their enlightenment. Their moment of comprehension grows out of retracing their own faulty process— whether in study, problem-solving, or reasoning—and receiving help in fixing it. Perhaps most important of all, communicate loudly and clearly that you don't consider failure a terminal condition, but rather a step along the way.

89.

Find a Trustworthy Confidant

Teaching is a tough job, no matter how rewarding. You're dealing with an academic discipline, but you are also dealing with people—your students, and sometimes their families, your colleagues, and your bosses and staff. At times, you will be taxed to your limits, and you will want to be able to talk about it.

However, teaching is also a job that calls for a high level of discretion. As a person in authority who is responsible for assessing the performance and behavior of others, you are privy to information that may be legally confidential. If not, it is, at least in ethical terms, privileged information. You may also find yourself in possession of a lot of personal information about the people that you teach or work with.

Whether you're dealing with student issues or concerns related to your colleagues, talking about your feelings can skate precariously close to indiscretion or gossip. As a teacher, you are part of a complex web—a community—and what you say and how you say it have a powerful effect on the whole.

It behooves anyone in the delicate situation of having confidential information and power over other people's lives to save some of their sharing for a special audience. Your institution probably provides forums for official discussions of problems. In addition, you and other faculty may meet regularly—either formally or informally—to talk through classroom challenges and individual cases that need attention. But there should be limits. Sharing concerns too easily slips into gossip, and gossip has a nasty habit of creating conflict and resentment. Try as you might, you sometimes cannot undo the negative effects of false information and miscommunication.

You are far better served keeping your professional conversations on a strictly professional level and your casual conversations free of information from your teaching exposure. Save the secrets for someone that you know you can trust without doubt. When you're grappling with privileged information, share it only with a trustworthy, objective confidant. The time may come when some issues need to be dealt with officially. If so, deal with them through proper channels and according to established protocols. You owe it to yourself to find someone who can listen. It's basic to mental and emotional health in a taxing, people-oriented profession. But you owe it to the people that you serve to make sure that the someone you choose is a worthy recipient.

90.

Do What You Say You'll Do

A successful teacher-student relationship depends largely on trust. You need to know that you can believe what your student tells you and rely on his or her good intentions in regard to schoolwork. Your student needs to know that when you say something, you mean it. Whether you're promising to return graded papers by a certain date, offering a special treat, or spelling out the consequences for misbehavior, your credibility is on the line. It only takes a few disappointments for your students to learn that they cannot trust what you say.

Your students listen more than you think, and they are waiting to see if you're the "real deal" or not. If you tell them that you'll return tests or papers to them by a certain date, make sure that you do it. Your insistence that they meet deadlines with assignments won't be particularly impressive if you don't manage to do the same. In fact, by your example, you'll convey the message that timely fulfillment of jobs doesn't matter. That's a poor lesson not only for education, but also for life.

If you promise a special event or treat, make sure that you spell out any qualifications ahead of time. If the event depends on good behavior or academic success, say so at the outset so that they know what they're choosing if they don't pull their weight. Don't spring it on them when it's too late for them to do anything about it. If there are potential problems outside of your control—for example, an official okay or the availability of transportation—let them know about those problems. If the disappointment comes, they will then understand that you didn't simply let them down or go back on your word.

When you deal with matters of behavior and performance, be diligent in making the rules clear. Young people and children, especially, feel strongly about issues of fairness. Woe unto the teacher who proclaims, "Do that again and you're out of here!" Unless that's a threat you intend to fulfill, those words come across as a sham. The next time that you speak, your students believe you a little less. Eventually, with enough idle threats, they won't believe you at all. When you deliver discipline unevenly, they'll be the first to cry foul, and rightly so. Whether you fail to follow through, hand down arbitrary punishments, or spring new rules on your students, you are betraying their trust.

Think before you say you will do something. When you do make a promise, spell out all the qualifiers. Most of all, do what you say you're going to do.

91.

Start on Time, Finish on Time

Your students learn more from what you do than what you say. And what you do communicates a great deal indeed, especially the way you treat the time that you have with your students. The way you arrive at your classroom sends your first clear message. If you arrive late, in a fluster, or ill-prepared, your students will logically conclude that you have other matters that you consider more important than them. You can't be bothered to do what it takes to be present and prepared in a timely manner, although they are expected to do so. If, on the other hand, you are waiting for the students when they arrive, with your materials organized and your spirit calmed, they understand at some level that you are invested in what you are doing and in them. They matter and your work with them is important.

In commencing, to dawdle, shuffle papers, or chitchat speaks of a lack of concern for the day's work and disrespect for your students' time. Older students in college and continuing education make sacrifices to be in your class and will hardly thank you for wasting the time that they've carved out of a busy schedule. Younger students generally attend school because they have to. While they may like the idea of playing their way through a class session instead of working, they will nonetheless react over time to a teacher who can't get it together to start promptly. Your nonchalance will translate into their indifference. After all, if you don't take it seriously, why should they? However, when you arrive on time and promptly begin class, your students understand that the class time is precious, that there's much to do and a limited amount of time in which to do it. Then when you call them to account for showing up late, you have a leg to stand on. Every minute they miss is meaningful time.

Ending on time may not seem as crucial as arriving and starting on time, but it is. You bolster morale when your students know that they can depend on a timely finish to the class period. Even the most interesting class can drag on a low energy or hard labor day. When the class continues past its dismissal time, your class becomes an irritation at best, a small torture at worst. Even more, your ability to bring your class period to a satisfying conclusion exemplifies the kind of self-discipline that you want to instill in your students.

Your handling of time in regard to class is an indicator to your students of your attitude toward your work and them. When you discipline yourself to start on time and end on time, you communicate not only respect for the class and your subject but also for the value of your students' time.

92.

Create Constructive Rituals

Human beings have a fundamental need for security. Until that need is met, they do not readily move on to meeting their social and intellectual needs. This is true in your classroom as surely as it is in the rest of their lives. When you create an environment that feels safe and predictable, you help equip your students for the task of learning, growing, and relating effectively to others.

One of the means through which people build a sense of security and safety is ritual. We ritualize important moments in our lives—births, religious confirmations, graduations, marriages, deaths—and they become benchmarks and foundations for new chapters. We ritualize the passage of time with weekends, vacations, holidays, and seasonal celebrations, and thus create a sense of anticipation that infuses our years. We even ritualize our daily schedules with set mealtimes and certain foods, as well as times for reading the paper, having a snack, or sitting down together. Our rituals give us a sense of security and belonging. We know what to expect, and we are disconcerted when the expected fails to happen.

The classroom provides ample opportunity for ritual. Certain jobs need to be done routinely—taking attendance, handing out papers, cleaning a blackboard, or raising or closing blinds. These can be turned into the mundane rituals that get your class going or keep your students physically involved in the "housekeeping." More creative activities, such as making decorative displays for various units of study, presenting interpretive projects on study material, or making regular visits to the school library for "research" days can also add a sense of tradition and expectation.

You can develop rituals around birthdays, holidays, or assembly days that students can count on. They'll know that when it's someone's birthday, for instance, that you always arrange for a fifteen-minute celebration with goodies and time off from studies. They'll come to expect that when the season changes, you'll decorate a certain display with colors and themes that are appropriate, or that when a school day is shortened for whatever reason, you'll use the shorter period in some unusual and engaging way.

What you ritualize is probably less important than the fact that you develop rituals. Rituals create bonds among the participants and give a sense of stability to the group and the environment.

93.

Regroup When You Need To

Sometimes, your best efforts cannot make a class go the way that you intended. You may be dealing with an unexpected interruption or upset. You may face a group that seems determined to act up. Or you may find that your plans simply didn't produce the response that you were counting on.

Because teaching is by definition a human enterprise, you might as well take these experiences in stride. People are flaky, and plans often go awry. Your best defense against plans that don't work is to be willing to stop and regroup. This means, of course, that you'll do yourself an enormous favor by keeping a stock of "plan B's" in your repertoire.

Backup plans may involve some tried-and-true methods of changing the pace and interest level of a class. A surprise class "bee" in which teams compete in a question-and-answer contest based on your material can shake everyone up. Build an oral quiz on the model of a baseball game, and you'll have a surprising amount of energy in a hurry. If you've successfully used creative lesson plans in the past, keep them in your back pocket for adaptation on the spot when a class is misfiring. Alternatively, when you have a number of different approaches to a given day's lesson, jot down the ideas that you have chosen not to use. In the event that your approach backfires, you can fall back on other ideas.

What you don't want to do is stare at a room full of glassy eyes, knowing that you might as well be talking to the wall. You don't want to proceed with a discussion in which you have inadvertently aroused animosity or resentment. When you sense that all is not well, make a quick assessment. If you can't pinpoint the problem, don't stress over it. Instead, be prepared to change the atmosphere with an unexpected question, a switch from books to paperwork, or from presentation to class participation. Don't be afraid to change tracks or tactics. It's all in a day's work for a good teacher, and it redeems time that would otherwise be lost.

94.

Lose the Savior Complex

M ost teachers, by nature and calling, have a desire to help the people that they teach. That's part of the impulse that leads them into such demanding work, despite relatively low pay scales and high expectations from others. They want to impart a body of knowledge and also take part in the personal development of their students. How their students fare, academically and otherwise, is a matter of concern and reward.

This is good news and bad news. The good news is that students of dedicated teachers are blessed with a guide and mentor at a time when they are primed to grow. The bad news is that the dedicated teacher sometimes takes on more of the job than is appropriate or effective. When a teacher crosses the line from helper to savior, even if only in his or her own mind, pitfalls multiply. Suddenly, the teacher-student relationship takes on do-or-die stakes, and the teacher's level of stress and frustration increases.

Take stock of how you understand your role in the lives of your students. No matter how it may seem to you, you are just one of many who share the responsibility for your students' best interests. Even if you limit your thinking to their academic needs—which you are unlikely to do, if you're devoted to your profession—there may be others available to nurture them.

Pay attention to the way that you think. When you hear yourself whispering, "It's up to me. I'm the only one who can help this person," it's time to take a step back for a reality check. Certainly, there will be times when you are a major player in a person's education and life, but you need to guard against ever buying into the savior role. It's not up to you. You are just a piece of the puzzle. You are responsible for your share of the job, not the whole job.

When you find yourself falling prey to this way of thinking, make a point of drawing other relevant players into the mix. It's a quick, straightforward way to remind yourself of the team on which you play. You can be instrumental in important ways, but you'll only shortchange your students if you don't support the network that shares the responsibility.

95.

Don't Be Tested by the Tests

Standardized testing has become a regular part of education, and for many teachers, enough is too much. Not only are students subjected to the traditional placement and entrance testing that has existed for many years. They now undergo regular competency testing also, the results of which can have serious implications for particular school systems, their funding, and their staff. The stakes seem high enough that parents are paying large sums of money to see their children adequately prepared for such testing by private agencies. And some teachers resent pressure from their supervisors to teach for the tests—to crowd routine curriculum in the interest of preparing students specifically for standardized tests.

Certainly, competency tests can act as guides to the relative ability of students to succeed in particular programs or in advanced degree work. It's also in the interest of identifying what ails the educational system or particular schools to apply some standardized testing. There's no question that public schooling has let us down in some critical regards, especially among specific socioeconomic groups. Some schools simply don't have the resources to meet the needs of the students in their community. Whether or not testing succeeds in precipitating positive change is open to debate. In the meantime, teachers at most levels are saddled with the tests and all the pressure, preparation, paperwork, and time that they entail.

If testing is the bane of your existence, it's time to come to grips with reality. This element of modern education is not going away anytime soon. If you are convinced that it is bad for your students or their education, by all means, make your voice heard in whatever way that you can. Organize, write petitions, participate in studies, form a lobby, and talk to your administrators.

Don't, however, let your frustration with one aspect of the system rob you of the joy of your profession or your commitment to your students. Unless big changes happen at the national level, your students will be expected to partake in the testing, and one of your responsibilities will be to prepare them. Have the wisdom to know what you can change and what you can't. Tackle the job with a good grace, and work to develop the most effective and efficient preparation that you can for your students. Don't waste your energy and resources on fussing and fuming. Trade negative emotions—which take their toll on you and your students—for positive action.

96.

Push the Paperwork off Your Desk

Procrastination probably causes more day-to-day stress than almost any other factor, if you happen to be someone who postpones the more mundane tasks of life. For the teacher, paperwork ranks high on the list of tedious details. Record-keeping, attendance, progress reports, homework, tests, essays, and other regular reports have a way of overloading the "in" basket.

If paperwork is your bugaboo, come to terms with it now. Reckon with the fact that paperwork is intrinsic to your job, like it or not—part of what you're paid to do. Perhaps you entered the teaching profession with romantic, idealistic expectations that your work life would be all people, progress, and successes. That's fine, but your expectations need to be honed by real life. Until you face the fact that you are responsible for the paperwork—that in fact it serves some very important functions—you'll suffer frustrations that have no relief.

Bring your perception of paperwork into proportion. It's only mountainous if you consistently postpone it. It's not an impossible task if you deal with it in daily small doses that keep the "out" basket as busy as the "in." You may find that if you get in the habit of keeping at it, the paperwork won't be nearly as much as you've come to believe.

Create a plan for doing your paperwork. People who have beaten clutter trouble in other areas of life have some wisdom to offer here. Almost universally, they've learned to set aside a small but quality chunk of time daily for staying ahead of the load. It's amazing, for instance, how much you can accomplish in just one half hour a day if you commit yourself to keeping that time free of other distractions and temptations. Consider it a date—your time for maintaining balance and sanity in your life.

You may think that you can't keep a half hour free of distraction. The word "can't" is your demon. Get rid of it, and make the time. Make paperwork the last thing that you do before leaving for work in the morning, leaving work at the end of the day, or turning off the light at night. Identify wasted time in your daily schedule and substitute the satisfying work of pushing the paperwork off your desk. Give it a chance and see if it doesn't relieve a lot of stress.

97.

Apologize

There are all sorts of reasons why teachers can find it difficult to apologize to their students. Pride, embarrassment, or self-righteousness can seal their lips, even when they know that they are wrong. Or they harbor the mistaken notion that apologizing undermines their authority. Nothing could be further from the truth. In fact, nothing undermines the teacher-student relationship as readily as a student's sense of being wronged.

Maybe you fly off the handle in the classroom, or you falsely accuse a student based on past experiences, faulty reports, or an incorrect perception. Perhaps you make a mistake in grading, or you fail to fulfill a promise. All of these situations are forgivable, and all are common occurrences for teachers. You are, after all, human. And human beings make mistakes.

Students are certainly capable of blaming you for things that are neither your fault nor your responsibility, but they are also capable of discerning when you have been at fault. If you refuse to own up or make amends, they will feel the injustice of it and learn to trust you less. Over time, you'll lose your credibility and your students' respect.

Step up to the plate when you've made a mistake or lost your cool. Promote personal responsibility in class. Every time that you face the music for your own frailties in relation to your students, you model that quality. An apology is nothing more than taking responsibility for your own mistakes. In effect, you say, "I respect myself and you enough to admit when I'm wrong." Instead of being diminished in your students' eyes, you'll find that they are far more likely to respect and support your efforts to be the best kind of teacher that you can be.

98.

Do Your Homework

Most teachers make a point of the need for students to do their work in a thorough and timely fashion. They know that one lesson builds on another, and that one missed assignment can quickly bog a student down. This is a crucial lesson for students if they're going to succeed in their education. It is also a critical life skill.

Unfortunately, some teachers don't practice what they preach. They depend on old lesson plans without bringing them up to date or adequately reviewing them. They fail to return homework, papers, tests, and projects promptly.

You can be sure, no matter how experienced you are, that if you aren't doing your homework, your studenets will know the difference. And the message they'll carry away is that your class is not worthy of your best efforts—or theirs.

When you come to class fresh, excited, and on top of your material and your approach, you show your students what learning means. At some level, they understand from your example that a quality education doesn't happen without effort and discipline.

99.

Listen

A teacher is assaulted by voices all day, every day. Listening to everyone may seem overwhelming by the time that you're facing the umpteenth student with something "important" to say. Don't despair. It doesn't matter whether you have a natural ability to listen well. Like all of the skills that you use to teach, effective listening can be learned—and bad habits from the past can be replaced with good ones now.

A number of factors play important roles in your ability to listen. First, you need to be present. This may sound obvious, but in truth, many of us "tune out" when it's time to listen. We may look like we're listening, but we're actually following our own thoughts down other paths. We may pick up enough of what the speaker says to respond reasonably well, but we've missed any deeper meanings. When you're listening to someone, make a point of looking at him or her. Pay attention to errant thoughts and distractions, and consciously push them to the side.

When you listen, you need to engage much more than your aural senses. Communication is far more complicated than words. Unless you look and listen at the same time, you will miss out on body language, facial expressions, posture, movements, and tone.

As you practice active listening, you'll find yourself able to empathize with the speaker. As long as you steadfastly maintain your own point of view, your ability to understand is hampered. The person you listen to has a perspective, too, and makes sense to him or herself. Listen with the intention of "getting" how the other person understands what he or she is saying. You don't have to agree; you just need to get it.

Finally, make your listening interactive. Test your understanding of what the other person is saying by restating it in your own words. Respond with nods, physical gestures, and eye contact, certainly, but also speak in turn—not in reference to yourself or others, but as a way of clarifying and repeating what you have heard.

Listening needs practice, just like any other skill. Once you start paying attention, you'll become more sensitive to the moments when you aren't listening well. Figure out what blocks your effective listening, and make a point of overcoming it.

100.

Let Every Day Be a New Beginning

Nothing takes the sunshine out of a new day like the clouds of the past. Don't let yesterday's problems and setbacks stop you from the fresh start that today offers. You are on a journey as a teacher. You don't arrive; you move along. You grow and develop, just like your students. Every day offers new opportunities for you to correct past mistakes, acquire new skills, build better relationships, and try out new ideas.

Past problems can turn into traps. They become little negative voices in your head that tell you that you can't do any better. They plant seeds of self-doubt and sap your creative energy. Don't give in to them! You have the power every day to do better. You can face your shortcomings honestly and do what's necessary to improve. You can face unsatisfactory relationships squarely and take steps to repair and rebuild them. You can face ongoing challenges courageously with the conviction that you've learned a lot about what doesn't work, and that you are closing in on what does.

The power of your attitude in each new day is incalculable. More often than not, the difference between a successful teaching experience and an unsuccessful one is not the experience itself, but rather the way that you look at it and what you do with it. When you get up and start a new teaching day, remind yourself that the day is yours to define. You can surrender yourself to the fates and be a victim of every unmet challenge, or you can seize this precious time that you've been given and make something extraordinary of it.

Start every day with gratitude for another day to fulfill your teaching mission. View it as an opportunity that is yours to own. The responsibility and the privilege are yours.